The *I love* Elvis cookbook

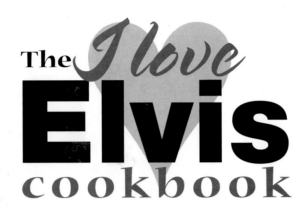

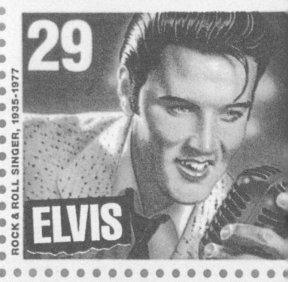

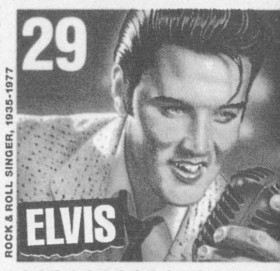

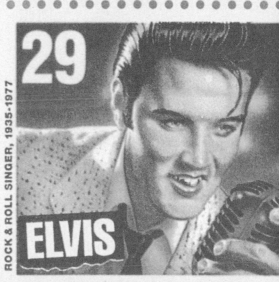

The *I love* **Elvis** cookbook

COURAGE
BOOKS

AN IMPRINT OF RUNNING PRESS
PHILADELPHIA · LONDON

CLB 4960
This edition first published in 1998 in the United States by Courage Books.
© CLB International
A division of Quadrillion Publishing Ltd, Godalming, Surrey GU7 1XW, England

Printed and bound in Singapore by Tien Wah Press.

9 8 7 6 5 4 3 2 1
Digit on the right indicates the number of this printing

Library of Congress Cataloging-in-Publication Number 97-68294

ISBN 0-7624-0276-8

This book was designed and produced by CLB International
Godalming, Surrey, England, GU7 1XW

Contributor (pages 6–11, 12, 26, 40, 54, 68 and captions to memorabilia): Mick Farren

Project management: Jo Richardson

Design: Liz Chidlow

Illustration: Philip Chidlow

Food photography: Amanda Heywood

Home economy: Elizabeth Wolf-Cohen

Memorabilia photography: Andrew Dee

Production: Ruth Arthur and Neil Randles

Color reproduction: HBM Print Ltd

Published by Courage Books, an imprint of Running Press Book Publishers
125 South Twenty-second Street
Philadelphia, Pennsylvania 19103-4399

CONTENTS

ELVIS HAS LEFT THE KITCHEN

In the winter of 1935, when Elvis Presley was born in near abject poverty, Tupelo, Mississippi may not have been the most wretched place on God's green earth but it was probably in the hot hundred of the most wretched in the United States. The Great Depression hit hard and mercilessly in the agricultural South, and newlyweds Gladys and Vernon Presley took more than their fair share of hard knocks. Vernon drifted from job to job and suffered long bouts of unemployment. As the constant struggle for survival continued through the late 1930s, the fortunes of the Presley family seemed to echo the old blues line, 'if it wasn't for real bad, I wouldn't have no luck at all.' In one ill-fated moment of desperation, Vernon Presley succumbed to the temptation to alter fraudulently a cheque for $4 to $40. For this $36 fraud, Elvis's father was sentenced to three years

in the Mississippi State Penitentiary at Parchman. While Vernon was doing time, Gladys and the three year-old Elvis were left to get by as best they could. While Elvis may not have ever actually starved, there were times when meals were not only meager but also plain and repetitive. These childhood experiences seem to have shaped his taste in food for the rest of his life.

The onset of World War II brought the Presley family some relief from the worst, with Vernon finding better jobs. After the war, when millions of demobilized GIs were thrown on the job market, things once again declined for Elvis and his parents. In 1948, Vernon decided to move the family to Memphis, hoping that the "big city" would offer better prospects. But the Presleys quickly qualified as tenants in Lauderdale Courts, a public-assisted housing project in downtown Memphis for families with a combined income of less than $2,500, demonstrating that their circumstances were only marginally improved.

Gladys seems to have made a practice of squirreling away some of the grocery money, so, although the usual family fare was pretty dull and minimal, she could, now and then, lay out a spread. Gladys Presley always talked about herself as a

"six eggs and two sticks of butter kind of cook." Elvis always went back to the memories of these childhood treats.

On first examination, it might seem strange that a man who, at the height of his popularity, was not only a multimillionaire but also beloved by half the teenage world, should cling almost desperately to the favorite foods of his childhood. The key to understanding Elvis, however, is that his life was totally unlike anyone else's to a degree that almost boggles the mind. Fame fell hard and fast on Elvis at a very early age, and as though from a great height. A poll in the mid '60s concluded that Elvis was one of the three most recognizable individuals on the planet, along with Chairman Mao and Muhammad Ali. Later, in the 1980s, the three global symbols became Jesus Christ, Elvis, and Coca Cola.

When other young men were taking their dates to restaurants and learning how not to be intimidated by waiters, Elvis remained trapped, a virtual prisoner, in his home or hotel. To venture forth from the closed and protected enclave of the moment meant running the gauntlet of marauding fans and gawkers. He reigned as king in the isolated environment of his own lonely kingdom surrounded by yes-man retainers and behive-haired beauty queens. His life was a paradox in which, on some levels, he would achieve a degree of lunatic sophistication, while on others, he simply never learned the basic ways of the world. He would happily spend some $40,000 to fly himself and his entourage from Memphis to Colorado to pick up peanut butter and jelly sandwiches from a delicatessen in Denver for which he had developed a momentary obsession. At the same time, he was pathologically reluctant to walk into a restaurant and order dinner, not only because of the risk

of potential fan hysteria, but also because he had never learned his way around a place setting.

The isolation of Elvis's life and the severe limitations in his ability to go out into the world also meant that he had little chance to experiment with different regional and national cuisines. In Germany, while doing his 1958 through 1960 stint in the military, he reportedly developed a taste for bratwurst and sauerkraut. Somewhere along the road, he developed a nodding acquaintance with Chinese food. By all accounts, he knew his way around a basic Italian

American menu and Marty Lacker, a long-time Presley retainer in the Memphis Mafia, also claims to have introduced him to the delights of Jewish deli. For the most part, though, Elvis Presley was an ultimately extreme creature of habit. He liked what he knew, and he knew what he liked—and, for the most part, what he liked was the same basic fare that Gladys served back home.

Although much has been exaggerated, there is no doubt that Elvis went on such mammoth eating binges that it could only indicate an individual who was looking for comfort rather than sustenance in food. Both the way he ate and what he ate had obvious roots in the circumstances of his childhood.

In interviews with the biographer Alanna Nash, Lamar Fike, another veteran of the Memphis Mafia, tells how "Elvis had very strange eating habits. In '56 and '57 he would eat sauerkraut, mashed potatoes and gravy, very crisp bacon, and tomatoes. He would crumble up the bacon and put it in the mashed potatoes and take the sauerkraut and gravy and make a mixture of it." According to Fike, Elvis would become completely obsessive about one specific dish. "He'd eat the same thing over and over again. He'd eat it until he couldn't stand it. Then he'd quit eating for a very long time. About eight months before he died, I looked up one day and he was back to mashed

potatoes and gravy and sliced tomatoes, and he was crumbling up burned bacon . . . God he loved bacon. He could eat a pound or a pound and a half of it at a time. But it had to be burned almost beyond recognition."

Bacon wasn't the only thing that Elvis liked overcooked beyond recognition. Marty Lacker recalls that he liked his eggs "fried so hard you could drive a nail through them.". . ."Any meat that Elvis ate had to be almost burnt. He didn't like to see any red or any blood. He'd gag at the sight of a pink hamburger. Or he'd throw it away or throw it at someone." Lamar Fike tells a similar story. "You could wear it for shoes, his meat was so tough."

For most traveling rock-and-roll bands, breakfast is the most important meal of the day. This was as true back in the 1950s as it is today in the 1990s.

Musicians roll out of bed to face a long day of traveling—boring hours staring out of the window of the plane, car, van, or tour bus. One of the obvious solutions is to eat a huge greasy breakfast and hope to go back to sleep. The pattern has become so standard that it has become a hallmark of the rock-and-roll touring ritual. While the roadies gathered up the luggage or gassed up the truck, the band would sit in the hotel coffee shop, hunched and maybe hung-over, with plates of eggs, bacon, pancakes, or French toast, and cups of the inevitable high-octane coffee or glass of Coca Cola in front of them.

This is exactly how Elvis Presley started his musical career and, once again, it created a pattern for the rest of his life. Even when he traveled from concert to concert in the Lisa Marie, the four-engined private jet named after his daughter, he still made sure that the galley was stocked with only slightly more upmarket versions of the truckstop and coffee shop fare.

It may seem weird to anyone who has ever been involved in the mechanics of live rock touring that Elvis, with all his money and seemingly unlimited control over his on-the-road lifestyle, never aspired to anything better than this enforced diet of the humblest struggling band. In this, however, Elvis was not unlike many other rock performers who have evolved odd obsessive quirks to counteract both the unreal demands and the crushing boredom of touring.

The root of the matter is that the rock-and-roll band is expected, night after night, to please a crowd by performing a special kind of creative magic. Although the mechanics of music may be fully understood, the X factor that gets the crowd screaming and on its feet is an ongoing mystery and the irrational fear, even for the greatest stars, is that somehow, one day, the magic will run out or cease to work. It's this fear that breeds behavior that might seem irrational or even demented to the outsider but makes absolute sense to those who are part of it. The rock band tends to become a tight knit group, a closed traveling enclave that sees itself as set apart from the rest of the normal world. They may quarrel with each other and fight among themselves, but they will also go to almost any lengths to preserve the fantasy that they are special individuals, men and women set apart from the routine, nine-to-five world. This sense of being a breed apart frequently leads to a kind of cowboy recklessness. In the short term, it can make the hardship tolerable. But, in many cases, it also plants the seeds of what has come to be known as rock-and-roll madness.

It's probably safe to say, without risking too many accusations of being disrespectful to the King, that Elvis had all the above in spades. The wrought iron gates and protective walls of Graceland, the guarded hotel suites, the ever-present buffer zone of good ol' boy henchmen who worked on the principle that no one came to Elvis except through them all served to make his sense of uniqueness watertight and total. His word was law inside his private domain, and things that would have seemed aberrant or even maniacal in an ordinary mortal were accepted as the norm. Elvis was the first and the greatest and, above all, larger than life. He had the credentials to be excessive in all things, and he may even have felt that excess was something expected of him. Everything he perceived confirmed this. With only a precious few exceptions, everyone who approached

Elvis was unable to act naturally. Even other established stars went into paroxysms of fawning flattery. Taken *en masse*, Elvis only saw crowds in the grip of mass insanity.

It was nothing short of a miracle that Elvis didn't develop a complete contempt for his fans and maybe humanity at large. Despite the lunacy that followed him everywhere, all accounts—even the most hostile—plainly indicate that Elvis maintained both a devotion and gratitude to his fans for putting him where he was.

It has to be said that some of Elvis's eating habits verged on the truly bizarre. We can't get around that but we can try to understand it. Elvis rose to fame and fortune in the United States of America in the 1950s—the greatest and most conspicuous consumer society the world had even seen. It's little wonder that Elvis felt the need to consume more conspicuously than anyone else around. The need to have more material things on every level was virtually a defining factor in Elvis's life. The unfortunate part was that Elvis had neither the experience nor self education to become truly creative in his consumption. He didn't spend his money on caviar or truffles. As far as caviar in particular was concerned, Elvis had a pathological loathing for the smell of fish and that was that. It might cost $2,000 an ounce, but it was still fish and therefore banished by the King.

Lamar Fike has already pointed out how Elvis would get on a kick for a certain dish. Some of these preoccupations, however, were to say the least strange. In 1966, Elvis briefly owned the Circle G Ranch, a 150-acre spread, across the stateline from Graceland, in Walls, Mississippi. After buying the ranch, Elvis became fascinated with the cowboy life and, dressed in full Roy Rogers western movie regalia, would ride the back forty of his palomino Rising Sun, accompanied sometimes by then bride-to-be Priscilla and always by two or more of the Memphis Mafia. Why shouldn't Elvis play cowboys on a grand scale—he had the money. What was less understandable was the habit he developed of eating plain hamburger or hotdog buns straight from the plastic supermarket package. For a month or more, Elvis went nowhere without his bag of bread. He even tied one to his saddle while riding and munched constantly.

Later, during the Vegas period, Elvis developed a profound craving for frozen popsicles. At 4 am, members of the Memphis Mafia recall being sent out into

the streets of Las Vegas to pick up a $100 worth of Popsicles, Dreamsicles, and Fudgesicles. Enough could never be enough for Elvis. He seems to have been constantly expecting famine. Graceland certainly appears to have been constantly stocked for a siege. Before Elvis went in the army, the cooking at Graceland was largely taken care of by Gladys, who so doted on her only surviving child that she personally made sure he lacked nothing. After he returned from military service and Gladys had passed away, the Graceland kitchen was put on a much more professional basis. It had a 24-hour staff and storage facilities that had to be prepared to handle all but the most perverse of Elvis's culinary whims at a moment's notice.

In any commentary on the life and tastes of Elvis Presley, it is impossible to avoid the dark side. After a full 20 years, the inevitable decline and fall casts a shadow over any retelling of the story. We protect ourselves from the unpleasant reality of the bloated and disorientated superstar by repeating the fat jokes or perhaps mailing out $10 to something like The Dead Elvis Fan Club for a package of tasteless, cheaply produced geegaws. That someone with the natural gifts of Elvis Presley could totally ruin and destroy himself by the age of 43 seems like such an artistic catastrophe that, rather than dwell on the reality, fans will tangent out into a doleful quasi religion, or maintain denial and claim he is still alive, living under the name John Burrows or some other pseudonym in Hawaii or Michigan.

The truth was Elvis always had something of a weight problem. Like his mother before him, he simply had a metabolism that caused him to put on pounds with unfortunate ease. He ate for pleasure and enjoyed the most fattening kinds of foods. He also tended to eat more when he was bored. In the golden days, before he went into the army, weight was really not a problem. He could eat what he liked because with a full schedule of stage shows, TV, and four movies to shoot, any excess fat was burned off by a combination of hard work and manic natural energy (and maybe with a little help from his mother's diet pills). It was only when he gave up

live performances and embarked on the Hollywood haul of increasingly unsatisfying moves that the problem began to reveal itself in public.

For Elvis to appear lean and beautiful, he needed to weigh in at somewhere around 150 pounds, but as early as 1963 to 1964, he would bulk up to more than 200 pounds between films. When it became time to return to the bikini beach and start yet another sun and fun picture, Elvis would go on a three to four week crash diet and shed anything from 30 or 40 pounds by fasting with the help of prescription amphetamines. Since he was rarely photographed during these 1960s eating binges, both fans and the movie

studio moguls were none the wiser. It was only around the time of the later moves—*Frankie and Johnny*, *Harum Scarum*, etc.—that the pills and fasting stopped doing the trick. Also, totally bored with making what seemed to be an endless procession of pointless and mindless films, Elvis also ceased to try so hard. It wasn't until the NBC TV special *Elvis*, the so-called comeback show, that his life was back on track.

For a while, between 1968 and 1970, Elvis was suddenly on form again. He was performing live again. His interest in music was rekindled. The bouts of overeating were pretty much under control, and he was using karate as a regular means of exercise. However, a couple of years after his return to the live stage he once again became bored with a routine that seemed to be going nowhere. Spending over two hundred days a year either touring or playing Las Vegas began to take its toll. The pills and the wild food binges started up again, and only the prospect of the satellite TV show *Aloha From Hawaii* in January 1973 provided enough incentive for him to pull himself together. Prior to *Aloha From Hawaii*, Lamar Fike, Marty Laker, and both Red and Sonny West joined Elvis in a drastic weight-loss program. "The doctor supplied the food, little bitty pieces of meat that you'd either boil in the package or eat dry. They'd be in the

kitchen in the suite in Vegas, boiling these things.". . . "We ate only 500 or 600 calories a day. My God, anyone could lose weight on that. Elvis got down to 175 or 180 pounds."

Unfortunately, immediately after the TV show was completed, Elvis went straight back to Las Vegas and the same way of life that would ultimately prove his downfall. In the four and a half years between *Aloha From Hawaii* and his death in August, 1977, no new source of inspiration appeared on the horizon. In the final days, on massive amounts of tranquilizers, pain killers, and sleeping pills, he would nod out while eating and one of the entourage would have to perform the Heimlich maneuver to stop him from choking. The ultimate irony was that Elvis died during yet another attempt at getting his weight down for the upcoming tour—the Tour That Never Was. "On August 14th, Elvis started on a sort of pre-tour fast to lose weight. Of course, he was leaving on the 16th, so that didn't give him a lot of time. But Elvis was the type of person who would go on a diet today and try to lose 50 pounds by one o'clock. At one point, I think he was eating nothing but low-cal Jell-O ten times a day."

As already noted, no commentary on the life, tastes, or behavior of Elvis Presley can ignore the dark side of his personality or the bleak end to the story. This is not to say, though, that we need to dwell unreasonably on the negative. If the election held by the US Postal Service back in 1992 proved anything, it was that Elvis fans prefer to remember the young Elvis—flamboyantly dressed, classically handsome, and with a sexual energy and charisma unrivalled before or since. Elvis may, at times, have become an overblown parody of himself. But even these scars on the legend can't detract from the impact he had and the pleasure he gave. The recipes in this book are designed as a tribute, a way of invoking the memory of the young singer who quite literally changed the world. They are also representative of a basic American cuisine—solid, appetizing, and without undue frills. They may not be health food but, for the one doing the cooking and for those who merely sit and eat, they are a sure fire, down-home crowd pleaser. For those who know Southern cooking, it can be a pleasant remembrance of meals past. For those who don't, it's an introduction to a whole mess of unique delights. For both, it's presented here with about the most solid cultural connection one could hope to find.

Put on the *Elvis's Number One Singles* CD, watch the video tapes of *Jailhouse Rock* or *King Creole*, and sit down to pork chops and gravy. About the only warning we need offer is, enjoy but just don't make a habit of it!

Mick Farren

"THEY CALL ME POOR BOY"

The style of house in Tupelo, Mississippi where Elvis Presley was born and raised was known as a shotgun shack. The joke was that "you could fire a shotgun in the front door and the pellets would come out of the back door without hitting anything." No greater symbol could be found to define a family as "dirt poor"—poor enough that getting enough to eat could be a constant heartache. When Gladys spent some of her hoarded grocery money and laid on one of her "spreads," it was a red-letter day in the life of the young Elvis. This was downhome Southern cooking—maybe fried chicken and mashed potatoes, everything smothered in gravy, followed by chocolate pudding and washed down with RC Cola. For the rest of his life, these foods would remain among his favorite things.

SOUTHERN HOME-FRIED CHICKEN
Makes 8 servings

Before fast-food deep frying days, chicken was pan fried in a deep cast-iron skillet in vegetable shortening. Using only chicken breasts and removing the skin allows the buttermilk to penetrate the pieces evenly, producing a crisp, golden chicken which would have made ideal fare for the "dinners-on-the-ground" or church picnics Elvis enjoyed with Gladys after Sunday services at the First Assembly of God. Serve with biscuits and coleslaw, or bean or potato salad.

1½–2 cups buttermilk

Salt

Ground black pepper

Cayenne pepper

8 chicken breast halves, skin removed

2 cups all purpose flour

3–4 cups white vegetable shortening, for frying

1. In a large baking dish, combine the buttermilk, 1 teaspoon of salt, ½ teaspoon of ground black pepper, and ¼ teaspoon of cayenne pepper. Add the chicken breasts, turning each piece to coat evenly, and cover tightly with plastic wrap.

Refrigerate for at for least 2 hours or up to 24 hours, turning once.

2. Put the flour, 1 teaspoon of salt, ½ teaspoon of black pepper, and ¼ teaspoon of cayenne in a heavy-duty, plastic freezer bag. Close the bag and shake to mix. Working with 2–3 chicken breasts at a time, drain lightly and drop into the seasoned flour. Twist the bag closed and shake to coat evenly. Remove the pieces to a wire rack over a baking sheet, shaking off any excess flour. Repeat with the remaining pieces.

3. Meanwhile, heat enough shortening to a depth of ½ inch in a 10- or 12-inch cast-iron skillet to 350°F. Carefully lower the chicken pieces, skin side down, into the oil. Cook, covered with a domed lid, for 8–10 minutes, until golden brown, rearranging the pieces if necessary to brown evenly. Turn the chicken and cook for 8–10 minutes more, uncovered, until well browned. Using tongs or a slotted spoon, remove to the rack to drain.

BUTTERMILK BISCUITS
Makes 1 dozen biscuits

This traditional biscuit has a moist, tender crumb which is absolutely addictive. Split open the biscuits hot from the oven and top with butter for a real treat. Serve with a plate of fried green tomatoes, tender sweet corn on the cob, or a bowl of cooked fresh-shelled peas, lima beans, or crowder peas for a classic southern lunch.

Vegetable oil spray or vegetable oil, for greasing

2 cups self-rising flour

1 tablespoon baking powder

1 tablespoon sugar (optional)

½ teaspoon salt

½ cup white vegetable shortening, cut into small pieces

⅔ cup buttermilk

Melted butter for brushing (optional)

1. Preheat the oven to 425°F. Lightly spray or grease a large, heavy baking sheet. In a large mixing bowl, stir together the flour, baking powder, sugar (if using), and salt.

2. Sprinkle the shortening over the flour mixture and, using a pastry blender or two knives scissor-fashion, cut in the shortening until the mixture resembles fine crumbs. Make a well in the center and pour in the buttermilk. Combine the buttermilk and flour mixture until a sticky dough forms.

A bolo tie from 1956, one of the earliest pieces of Elvis merchandizing.

3. Turn out the dough onto a lightly floured work surface and knead lightly 4–5 times, until just blended. Roll out the dough about ½-inch thick.

4. Using a floured 2-inch plain biscuit or cookie cutter, cut the dough into as many rounds as possible using a straight downward motion; do not twist the cutter or the sides of the biscuits will not rise evenly. Alternatively, cut into 2-inch squares. Place the rounds on the baking sheet about 1 inch apart. If you prefer the biscuits with a very soft edge, place them close together on the baking sheet.

5. Knead the dough trimmings together lightly, reroll, and cut out as before. Bake for 10–12 minutes, or until golden. If you like, brush the tops with a little melted butter and serve hot from the oven.

PEANUT-STUFFED PORK CHOPS
Makes 4 servings

Pork chops were one of Elvis's favorite foods. Meat was not often on the menu in the early days at Tupelo, but when there was a little extra money, pork chops were the family choice. They were probably battered and fried to death in an old cast-iron skillet, quite unlike this upmarket version. I bet he'd love these stuffed with another favorite—peanuts.

½ cup fresh bread crumbs

½ cup green onions, minced

1 small dessert apple, peeled, cored, and finely chopped

½ cup dry roasted peanuts, coarsely chopped

2 tablespoons chopped fresh parsley

1 teaspoon dried sage

½ teaspoon dried thyme

½ teaspoon dry mustard powder

¼ teaspoon hot pepper sauce

4–5 tablespoons peanut oil

Salt and freshly ground pepper

4 loin pork chops, at least 1-inch thick

1 cup chicken stock or water, or half apple juice and stock or water

¼ cup heavy cream

1 tablespoon smooth peanut butter

1. To prepare the stuffing, put the first 9 ingredients in a bowl and add about 2 tablespoons of the peanut oil. Combine with a fork until well blended and the stuffing just holds together. Season and add a little stock or water if necessary.

2. Put the pork chops on a cutting board and trim off all but a very thin layer of fat. Using a thin, sharp knife, make a 'pocket' in each chop by cutting horizontally into the center from the outer edge to the bone, trying to keep the cut centered. Using a spoon, divide the mixture evenly among the chops.

3. In a heavy-bottomed frying pan or skillet, heat 2 tablespoons of the remaining oil over medium-high heat. When the oil is very hot, add the chops. Cook for 1–2 minutes. Using a pancake turner and a long-bladed metal spatula, carefully turn the chops. Cook for 1–2 minutes, until only just browned.

4. Remove to a plate and add the chicken stock, water, or apple juice to the pan, stirring to scrape up any browned bits on the bottom. Bring to a boil and skim off any fat or foam. Reduce the heat to low and return the chops to the pan. Cook, covered, for 25–30 minutes, until just cooked, basting occasionally.

5. Remove the chops to a serving dish and keep warm. Stir in the cream and peanut butter. Increase the heat to medium-high, bring to a boil, stirring constantly, and pour over the chops.

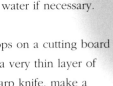

DOWN-HOME SMOTHERED RABBIT
Makes 4 servings

The Presleys, like most others in Northeastern Mississippi, were country folk. Elvis and Gladys must have jumped for joy when Vernon came home with a shot gun in one hand and a fresh young rabbit or squirral in the other.

¼ cup light soy sauce

2 tablespoons sweet chili sauce

1 tablespoon brown sugar

1 teaspoon mild chili powder (optional)

1 teaspoon dried sage, thyme, or oregano

2–3 pound rabbit, cut into pieces

1 cup all-purpose flour

Salt and freshly ground black pepper

Peanut or vegetable oil, for frying

2 large onions, thinly sliced into rings

2 cloves garlic, minced

1 cup dry white wine or apple cider

1 cup chicken stock

1 tablespoon finely shredded fresh sage or 2 tablespoons parsley

1. In a large baking dish, combine the soy sauce, chili sauce, brown sugar, chili powder (if using), and herbs. Add the rabbit pieces, turning to coat evenly.

2. Marinate for at least 2 hours or overnight. Put the flour, 1 teaspoon of salt, and ½ teaspoon of pepper into a heavy-duty freezer bag, close the bag, and shake to mix well. Taking 2–3 pieces of rabbit at a time, drain lightly, and drop into the seasoned flour. Twist the bag closed and shake to coat evenly. Shake to remove any excess flour and remove to a plate. Repeat with the remaining pieces.

3. Meanwhile, over medium-high heat, heat oil ¼-inch deep in a 10- or 12- inch heavy-bottomed frying pan or skillet. When the oil is very hot, but not smoking, carefully lower in the rabbit pieces—you may need to work in batches. Cook until well browned on both sides, turning once, for 10 minutes. Remove to a plate and set aside.

4. Pour off all but 2–3 tablespoons of the oil and return to a medium-low heat. Add the onions to the frying pan or skillet and cook until softened and beginning to turn golden. Add the garlic, wine or cider, stock, and any remaining marinade and bring to a boil over medium heat, stirring up any brown bits from the bottom. Skim off any foam which rises to the surface.

5. Return the rabbit pieces to the pan, spooning the onions and gravy over the pieces to coat well. Simmer over low heat for about 45 minutes, until tender, turning and basting occasionally. Sprinkle with the fresh herbs.

OLD-FASHIONED MEATLOAF
Makes 6–8 servings

Meatloaf began to appear on American tables just after the turn of this century, when hamburgers were becoming a staple of the "workman's" diet. Nowadays, meatloaf is a mainstay of American home cooking. In Elvis's youth, any beef was an extravagance and stretching a pound of ground beef with a few vegetables, oatmeal, or bread crumbs and eggs was a practical and economic addition to a poor boy's diet.

Vegetable oil spray or vegetable oil, for greasing

I cup rolled oats

½ cup whipping cream or half-and-half

2 tablespoons butter

I large onion, chopped

2 garlic cloves, finely chopped

2 stalks celery, finely chopped

2 pounds ground beef

I pound ground pork or bulk sausage meat

2 eggs, lightly beaten

½ cup chopped fresh parsley

1 teaspoon dried thyme

1 teaspoon dried sage

1½ teaspoons salt

I teaspoon freshly ground black pepper or ½ teaspoon hot pepper sauce

½ tablespoon Worcestershire or soy sauce

½ cup tomato sauce or tomato ketchup, plus extra for glazing

6 slices bacon, flattened with a knife

1. Preheat the oven to 350°F. Spray a large jelly roll pan with a vegetable spray or brush with oil. Put the rolled oats in a bowl and stir in the cream or half and half until combined. Set aside.

2. In a medium frying pan over medium heat, heat the butter. Add the onion and cook, stirring, for about 5 minutes, until softened and translucent. Stir in the garlic and celery and cook for 2 more minutes, stirring frequently. Set aside.

3. In a large mixing bowl with a fork or with your fingers, combine the beef and pork or sausage meat. Using a large wooden spoon or your hands, stir in the remaining ingredients, except the bacon slices, until just blended. Add the cooled onion mixture and reserved rolled oats and cream, and mix lightly to combine. Do not overwork the mixture or it will be too compact.

4. Shape the meat mixture into an oval loaf and set on the jelly roll pan. Lay the bacon strips crosswise over the loaf, tucking the ends under the edges of the loaf. Brush with a little extra tomato sauce or ketchup.

5. Bake the meat loaf for 1–1¼ hours, until well browned, glazing with the juices and drippings in the pan and brushing with a little more tomato sauce or ketchup if you like. Remove from the oven and allow to stand for about 10 minutes before slicing. You can use the drippings to make a gravy.

SOUTHERN-STYLE COLLARD GREENS

Makes 4 servings

6 ounces salt pork, diced

1 teaspoon salt

1 teaspoon sugar

2 pounds fresh collard, turnip, or mustard greens, very well washed

Hot pepper sauce, to taste

Vinegar, to taste

Southern Cornbread, for serving

1. Fill a large, heavy stockpot with 2 quarts of cold water. Add the salt pork, salt, and sugar and bring to a boil over medium-high heat. Skim off any foam and fat which rises to the surface. Simmer for 30 minutes.

2. Stir the greens into the simmering liquid, cover, and simmer for about an hour over low heat. Spoon into shallow bowls with some of the "pan-likker" and a dash of hot sauce and vinegar, and serve with Southern Cornbread.

SOUTHERN CORNBREAD

Makes one 10-inch loaf

Southern cornbread is traditionally baked in a heavy, black iron skillet, and served with collard greens to mop up the "pan-likker." The batter is made, then added to sizzling bacon drippings or lard melted in a hot skillet. It is then baked to a golden brown and served warm. Elvis loved butter and would have substituted it for bacon drippings.

8 tablespoons (1 stick) butter, cut into pieces

1¼ cups yellow or white cornmeal

¾ cup all-purpose flour

¼ cup sugar

2½ teaspoons baking powder

½ teaspoon salt

1 cup buttermilk

1 egg, lightly beaten

1. Preheat the oven to 425°F. Put the butter in a 9-or 10-inch heavy iron skillet and set it in the oven for 3–5 minutes, until melted. Swirl to coat the pan.

2. In a large mixing bowl, stir together the cornmeal, flour, sugar, baking powder, and salt and make a large well in the center. Pour all but 2 tablespoons of the melted butter into a 2-cup measure or medium bowl, and cool slightly. Keep the remaining butter and skillet warm. Using a fork, beat together the buttermilk, egg, and reserved butter. Pour into the well in the cornmeal-flour mixture and stir gently until just combined—do not overbeat. Pour the batter into the hot skillet.

3. Bake for 18–20 minutes, until a cake tester or wooden toothpick inserted in the center comes out clean and the cornbread is golden brown.

CHEESY GRITS CASSEROLE
Makes 6 servings

Satisfying and substantial grits became a staple of Elvis's diet when his father was sent to prison for forging a check for the sale of a pig! For three years, Elvis and his mother Gladys survived on grits, cheese, and locally grown vegetables from neighbors. Grits are made from finely ground, dried hulled white corn kernels, called hominy.

Vegetable oil spray or vegetable oil, for greasing

2 cups milk

2 cups water

¾ teaspoon onion salt

I cup regular grits

8 tablespoons (I stick) butter

1½ cups (6 ounces) shredded cheddar or Monterey Jack cheese

3 eggs, lightly beaten

4–5 green onions (scallions), finely chopped

Cayenne pepper or hot pepper sauce, to taste

Paprika

I. Preheat the oven to 350°F. Lightly grease a 1-quart baking dish. Put the milk, water, and onion salt in a large heavy-bottomed saucepan. Bring to a boil over medium-high heat. Gradually whisk in the grits and bring back to a boil. Reduce the heat to low and cover, simmering very gently for 12–15 minutes, until the grits are thickened, stirring frequently to prevent scorching.

2. Remove from the heat and stir in the butter and 1 cup (4 ounces) of the cheese, stirring until melted. Stir a large spoonful of grits into the beaten eggs and return the egg mixture to the green onions (scallions) and thickened grits, stirring vigorously. Season with cayenne pepper or hot pepper sauce.

3. Pour the mixture into the baking dish and bake for 25–30 minutes, until just set and golden. Sprinkle with the remaining cheese and bake for 5 minutes longer, until the cheese has just melted. Sprinkle with paprika and serve.

GOOD OLE PAN GRAVY
Makes about 2 cups

Contrary to popular belief, Elvis was not obsessive about gravy on everything unless, as in later years, he was away from home. He did take a little pan gravy on his mashed potatoes, and did love onion gravy and often requested it on his hamburgers. Good gravy relies on pan drippings. A good stock or broth also helps, but since this wasn't often available, milk, water, or even coffee was used to deglaze the pan.

2–3 tablespoons meat or bacon drippings

1 small onion, finely chopped (optional)

1–2 tablespoons all-purpose flour

2 cups water and/or stock and/or milk

Salt and freshly ground black pepper

Mashed potatoes, to serve (page 74)

1. Remove the pan-fried meat (chicken, pork chops, steak, or bacon) from the pan. Set aside and keep warm. Pour off all but 2–3 tablespoons of the drippings. Keep the skillet over medium heat.

2. If you like an onion-flavored gravy, add the chopped onion and using a wooden spoon, stir into the remaining drippings, scraping the bottom of the pan to release some of the browned bits. Add the flour and stir until it is golden and well blended.

3. Begin adding the liquid slowly, about ½ cup at a time, until it thickens, whisking constantly. Add more liquid, letting the gravy boil and thicken little by little; this prevents the gravy from lumping. Continue until all the liquid has been added, stirring frequently.

4. Reduce the heat to medium-low and let the gravy simmer until very thick. If you like a thin gravy, add more liquid; for a thicker gravy, continue cooking until the gravy reduces to the desired thickness. Do not season until the gravy has reached the desired thickness or it may taste too salty. Season with salt and

pepper and serve steaming hot. If you like a smooth gravy, strain before serving.

Variation

For a real Onion Gravy, make the pan gravy as above. In another skillet, fry 2 medium onions, thinly sliced in rounds, in 2 tablespoons of butter over medium-low heat for about 15 minutes, until golden and soft. Stir into the strained gravy and serve hot.

RICH-RED DEVIL'S FOOD CAKE
Makes 8 servings

This is one of the most popular cakes around, and no wonder. Rich, dark, chocolate layers sandwiched with a gooey fudgy chocolate icing, this is the kind of cake that would have been welcome at any church supper or picnic anywhere.

DEVIL'S FOOD CAKE

Butter or margarine, for greasing

1 cup plus 2 tablespoons unsweetened cocoa powder

½ teaspoon salt

1 cup plus 2 tablespoons boiling water

¾ cup (1½ sticks) unsalted butter or margarine

3 cups packed light brown sugar

3 eggs, lightly beaten

2 teaspoons vanilla extract

1½ cups buttermilk

2½ teaspoons baking soda

3 cups cake flour sifted

FUDGY CHOCOLATE FROSTING

2 cups sugar

½ teaspoon salt

3 ounces (3 squares) unsweetened chocolate, chopped

1 cup milk

2 tablespoons corn syrup

½ cup (1 stick) unsalted butter, cut into pieces

2 teaspoons vanilla extract

1. To prepare the cake layers, preheat the oven to 350°F. Lightly grease three 8-inch cake pans. Line the bottoms with nonstick baking parchment and grease again. Dust lightly with flour.

2. Put the cocoa and salt in a small bowl and slowly whisk in the boiling water until the cocoa dissolves and forms a paste. Set aside to cool.

3. In a large mixing bowl, using an electric mixer, beat the butter or margarine until creamy. Add the sugar and beat for 2–3 minutes, until light and fluffy. Gradually beat in the eggs until blended, then beat in the vanilla extract.

4. Put the buttermilk in a small bowl and stir in the baking soda—it will begin to fizz. Add ½ cup of the flour to the butter-egg mixture, stirring to blend, then add about ⅓ cup of the buttermilk mixture and stir to blend. Continue to add the flour and buttermilk alternately, blending well after each addition. Gradually stir in the cocoa mixture and stir until combined.

5. Divide the batter between the two pans and bake for 25–30 minutes, until a cake tester or wooden toothpick inserted in the center comes out clean. Remove the cakes to a wire rack to cool for 5 minutes, then unmold onto a wire rack.

6. To prepare the frosting, put the sugar, salt, and chopped chocolate in a heavy-bottomed medium saucepan. Slowly stir in the milk until well blended. Add the corn syrup and butter and bring to a boil over medium-high heat, stirring occasionally to help dissolve the sugar. Boil for 1 minute, stirring vigorously. Remove from the heat and cool slightly. Stir in the vanilla extract. When cool, whisk until thick and use immediately.

7. Remove the paper from the bottom of each cake layer, place 1 layer on a serving plate, and cover with about a quarter of the frosting. Top with the second cake layer, cover with another quarter of the frosting, and cover with the third cake layer, top side up. Frost the top and side of the cake. Serve at room temperature.

The Elvis Zippo, an odd memento for someone who rarely smoked!

PECAN PIE
Makes one 9-inch pie

PIECRUST

2 cups all-purpose flour, sifted

½ teaspoon salt

1½ cups (1 stick) unsalted butter, cut into small pieces

3 tablespoons white vegetable shortening, chilled

4–6 tablespoons iced water

Vegetable oil spray or vegetable oil, for greasing

FILLING

3-3½ cups pecan halves

3 eggs, lightly beaten

1 cup packed dark brown sugar

½ cup corn syrup

Grated zest and juice of ½ lemon

4 tablespoons butter, melted

2 teaspoons vanilla extract

1. Combine the flour and salt in a bowl. Sprinkle over the butter and shortening. Using fingertips, cut in the fats until the mixture resembles fine crumbs.

2. Sprinkle the iced water onto one area at a time, using a fork to mix. Continue adding water a tablespoon at a time, mixing to moisten the mixture. Add just enough to make the dough hold together. Pull the moistened dough to one side and form into a rough ball.

3. Turn out onto a large sheet of plastic wrap and, using the wrap as a guide, knead gently 4–5 times, until blended. Flatten into a disc shape, wrap well, and refrigerate for 30–40 minutes or overnight. Soften at room temperature before rolling.

4. Spray a 9-inch pie plate with a vegetable spray or brush lightly with oil. Unwrap the dough and place on a lightly floured work surface. Roll out the dough from the center toward the edge, turning it a quarter turn as you roll to keep it round, until ⅛-inch thick.

5. Roll the dough over the rolling pin and unroll over the pie plate. Trim off the excess, leaving a 1-inch overhang. Fold this under and pinch to form a stand-up edge.

Crimp the edge. Prick the bottom with a fork and refrigerate for 30 minutes.

6. Preheat the oven to 350°F. Pick out about 1 cup of perfect pecans and set aside. Coarsely chop the remaining nuts.

7. In a mixing bowl, using an electric mixer, beat the eggs and sugar until lightened. Beat in the corn syrup, lemon zest and juice, butter, and vanilla. Stir in the chopped pecans. Pour into the pie plate and set on a baking sheet.

8. Arrange the pecan halves on top of the filling. Bake for 40–45 minutes, until the filling is set and slightly puffed and the top is browned.

CHOCOLATE PUDDING
Makes 4–6 servings

Elvis isn't the only one who loved chocolate pudding!

²/₃ cup sugar

¼ cup cornstarch

¼ teaspoon salt

¼ teaspoon ground cinnamon (optional)

1 cup thick whipping cream

4 tablespoons (½ stick) butter or margarine

3½ ounces (3½ squares) unsweetened chocolate, chopped

1 egg

1 teaspoon vanilla extract

Whipped cream and chocolate shavings, to serve

1. In a large, heavy-bottomed saucepan, combine the sugar, cornstarch, salt, and cinnamon, if using. Gradually whisk in the cream to form a thick paste. Add the butter or margarine and chopped chocolate and set over medium heat. Cook until the chocolate melts and the mixture thickens, stirring frequently. Bring to a boil and boil for 1 minute, stirring constantly. Remove from the heat.

2. In a small bowl with a whisk or fork, beat the egg. Stir a spoonful of the hot chocolate mixture into the egg with the vanilla extract, whisking constantly. Slowly pour the egg mixture back into the chocolate mixture, whisking constantly to prevent the custard from lumping—the mixture will be very thick.

3. Press the mixture through a sieve into a 4-cup measure or pitcher.

4. Pour the pudding into 4–6 custard cups, ramekins, or dessert dishes. Cool, then refrigerate, covered, for about 2 hours or overnight, until well chilled. Serve with whipped cream and a few chocolate shavings on top.

The sleeve of Elvis's first ever EP, which came out in 1956.

"THERE'S GOOD ROCKIN' TONIGHT"

The life of a band on tour consists of long hours of waiting, punctuated by a brief interlude of intense excitement on stage. Very few performers eat in the hours immediately before a show. After the show, when normal people have retired to their beds or the television late show, the choice is limited to neon nighthawk, 24-hour fast food. The one thing that made life on the road a little more tolerable back in the 1950s, when Elvis, Scotty, and Bill played honky tonks and high school gyms, was the fast food. At that time, eating on the road was a matter of pulling into the "mom and pop" truckstop or diner. In many respects, the menu in those greasy spoons of yesteryear was an extension of basic family fare.

FRENCH TOAST

Makes 2 servings

2–3 eggs

1/4 cup milk

2 tablespoons honey

1/4 teaspoon salt

1/4 teaspoon cinnamon

Grated zest of 1/2 orange

1/2 teaspoon vanilla extract

4 slices white bread, sliced about 1/2-inch thick

2–3 tablespoons butter, for frying

Honey or maple syrup, to serve

1. In a shallow baking dish, large enough to hold the bread slices in one layer, beat the eggs with the next 6 ingredients.

2. Dip the bread into the egg mixture, turn, and dip the other side. Leave to absorb the egg mixture, turning once.

3. Heat the butter in a large skillet or griddle over medium-high heat. Add the bread and cook for 2–3 minutes, until golden. Turn and cook for about 1 minute more, until well browned.

BLUEBERRY PANCAKES

Makes about 1 dozen

Pancakes are one of those all-day breakfast choices on most roadside restaurant menus.

1 1/4 cups all-purpose flour

1/2 teaspoon baking powder

1/2 teaspoon baking soda

1/4 teaspoon salt

1 cup buttermilk

1/2–3/4 cups milk

1 tablespoon honey or sugar

2 tablespoons butter, melted

1/2 teaspoon vanilla extract

1/2 cup fresh blueberries

Melted butter, for cooking

Butter and maple syrup, to serve

1. In a large mixing bowl, stir together the flour, baking powder, baking soda, and salt. Make a well in the center.

2. In a 2-cup measure or pitcher, whisk together the buttermilk, 1/2 cup milk, the honey or sugar, melted butter, and vanilla extract. Pour into the well in the flour mixture and, using a wire whisk or fork, stir just until combined, adding a little more milk if the batter is too thick. Do not overbeat—a little unblended flour will not matter. Stir in the blueberries.

3. Put a large skillet or griddle (preferably nonstick) over medium heat and brush with a little melted butter. Drop the batter by large spoonfuls onto the hot skillet or griddle and cook for about 1 minute, until the edges are set and surface is covered with bubbles.

4. Turn and cook for another 30 seconds, until just golden on the bottom. Transfer to a heatproof plate or baking sheet and keep warm in a medium-low oven. Continue making pancakes until all the batter is used. Serve hot, topped with butter and maple syrup.

PORK 'N' HERB SAUSAGE PATTIES
Makes 12 patties

Almost all the old roadhouse cafés made their own sausage patties. Pork is probably the most important source of protein in the southern United States, and just about every part of the little piggy is used. Nowadays, ground lean pork is widely available in supermarkets.

1½ pounds lean ground pork

⅓ cup fresh white bread crumbs

I large egg, lightly beaten

2 green onions (scallions), finely chopped

2 teaspoons chopped fresh sage leaves or I teaspoon dried sage

2 tablespoons freshly chopped parsley

½ teaspoon hot pepper sauce

½ teaspoon ground allspice

Salt and freshly ground black pepper

Bacon drippings or vegetable oil, for frying

1. Put the ground pork in a large mixing bowl and add all the remaining ingredients except the bacon drippings or oil. Using a fork or your fingers, gently mix until just combined.

2. Working with wet hands, shape the mixture into twelve 2½-inch patties. Arrange on a baking sheet and refrigerate, covered, for at least 30 minutes or overnight.

3. In a large, heavy-bottomed skillet or griddle, heat 2 tablespoons of bacon drippings or oil over medium heat. Add the patties to the pan and cook for about 10 minutes, until the meat is cooked through and the patties are crisp and brown, turning at least once. Do not overcrowd—if necessary, cook in 2 batches and keep warm in a medium oven. Drain on paper towels and serve hot with Fried Cornmeal Mush (page 35) or scrambled or fried eggs.

Elvis enjoys lunch on the set of Jailhouse Rock. *Later in his life, few pictures would ever be published of Elvis eating after he became sensitive about his weight.*

DELUXE GRILLED CHEESE AND BACON SANDWICHES
Makes 4 sandwiches

Sandwiches were always available "on the road," although probably not as delicious as this one. Most of these "grilled cheese sandwiches" were made with commercial process cheese like Velveeta; this uses Gruyère or Monterey Jack.

8 tablespoons (1 stick) butter, softened

2 tablespoons Dijon-style mustard

1 tablespoon finely minced thyme leaves

1 tablespoon freshly chopped parsley

Freshly ground black pepper

8 slices firm white bread

½ pound cheddar, Gruyère, or Monterey Jack cheese, thinly sliced

½ pound bacon (at least 12 slices), cooked until crisp and drained

1–2 large tomatoes, thinly sliced

1 small red onion, thinly sliced

Vegetable oil spray or vegetable oil

1. In a small bowl with a wooden spoon, cream the butter, mustard, thyme, and parsley until well blended. Season with freshly ground black pepper.

2. Arrange the slices of bread on a work surface and spread very lightly with half the butter mixture. Divide half the cheese between 4 of the bread slices. Top each with 4 slices of crispy bacon—trim to fit if necessary. Cover each with tomato and onion slices, then top each with the remaining cheese slices and cover with the remaining 4 bread slices. Spread the remaining herb butter on the outside of the sandwich tops and bottoms.

3. Spray a large nonstick skillet or griddle with a vegetable oil cooking spray or brush lightly with oil. Set over medium heat until hot. Add the sandwiches (work in batches if necessary), and cook for about 3 minutes, until the bottoms are golden and crisp. Carefully turn the sandwiches and cook for about 3 minutes more, until golden and the cheese is just melted. Remove to a work surface, cut in half, and serve immediately.

THE FAMOUS FRIED PEANUT BUTTER-AND-BANANA SANDWICH
Makes 1 for Elvis

By 1956, Elvis was on the road for longer periods at a time and missed Gladys's home cooking. He missed his favorite snack, and when he got back home, Gladys would make and serve it any time of the day or night.

2 slices firm home-style white bread

4 tablespoons peanut butter

1 medium banana, thinly sliced

1 tablespoon oil

4 slices bacon

2 tablespoons butter or margarine, softened

Lettuce leaves and southern-style sweet pickle such as watermelon rind or sweetcorn relish, to serve

1. Place the bread slices on a work surface and spread both slices with the peanut butter. Cover 1 slice with the banana slices.

2. Heat the oil in a heavy-bottomed frying pan over medium-high heat. Add the bacon slices and cook for 3–5 minutes, until very crisp, turning once. Remove to a paper towel to drain and pour off all but 1 tablespoon of the bacon drippings from the pan. Layer the crisp bacon over the banana slices and top with the second bread slice, peanut butter side down, pressing lightly to seal.

3. Butter the outside of each bread slice and carefully add to the frying pan. Fry for about 2 minutes, until the bottom is brown and crisp. Turn and fry for 2 minutes more, until the bananas and peanut butter are just beginning to soften. Remove to a cutting board and slice in half. Arrange on lettuce leaves and serve hot with a favorite relish.

A selection of very early memorabilia, including the very first collection of Elvis's music and lyrics and the first set of Elvis bubble gum cards.

THE ELVIS BURGER
Makes 4 servings

Elvis's love affair with the hamburger probably began in his early youth in Tupelo, where hamburgers were early diner fare. Elvis used to save up and walk miles to one of the few diners serving burgers. This is probably a more deluxe version than the plain simple ones available in the 1940s in Tupelo.

1 pound 12 ounces ground beef

Salt and freshly ground black pepper

8 slices bacon, cut in half

4 slices cheddar or Monterey Jack cheese

4 burger buns, split and toasted

Lettuce leaves, sliced onion, ketchup, mayonnaise, or other favorite condiments, to serve

1. Put the beef in a large bowl and season with salt and pepper. Toss lightly to mix and shape into 4 large patties. Refrigerate until ready to use.

2. Lay the bacon slices in a large, heavy-bottomed frying pan and set over medium-high heat. Cook for 5–8 minutes, until very crisp (Elvis loved burnt bacon!), turning once. Remove the bacon to a paper towel to drain.

3. Pour off all but 2 tablespoons of the bacon drippings and return the pan to the heat. Add the hamburgers to the hot pan and cook for 6–8 minutes, or longer for more well-done burgers, turning once. One minute before the end of the cooking time, top each burger with a slice of cheese to soften.

4. Arrange the lettuce on the burger bun bottoms and transfer each burger to a lettuce-lined bun. Top each burger with 2 slices of bacon, sliced onion, ketchup, or any other condiments. Cover with the top of the bun and serve immediately. Serve with French fries.

Tip

Alternatively, to barbecue or grill the burgers, prepare a charcoal, gas, or electric barbecue or preheat a kitchen grill. Arrange the patties on an oiled rack or a greased, foil-lined grill pan and cook for 6–8 minutes, or until the desired degree of doneness is reached.

FRENCH FRIES
Makes 4 servings

5–6 Large potatoes

Vegetable oil, for frying

Salt

1. Trim each potato into a square-sided shape. Cut lengthways into ½-inch slices, then stack and cut the slices into ½-inch sticks. Rinse the potatoes in cold water and dry well in a clean tea towel.

2. Pour at least 3 inches of oil into a deep saucepan or deep-fat fryer and heat to 325°F, or until a cube of bread browns in 30 seconds. Fry in batches for 5–6 minutes, until tender and just beginning to brown. Remove with a slotted spoon and drain on paper towels.

3. Just before serving, reheat the oil to the hotter temperature of 375°F, and refry for 2–3 minutes, until crisp and golden. Remove and drain on paper towels. Sprinkle with salt and serve while hot.

A comparatively recent enamel Elvis pin featuring a 1950s-style jukebox.

BAR-B-QUE RIBS
Makes 4 servings

"Barbecue," as it's called, is an institution all over the South, each state claiming it serves the best. Make this easy barbecue sauce or buy a good commercial sauce if you feel really lazy. Barbecue is traditionally served with coleslaw and sour pickles.

EASY BARBECUE
SAUCE

2 tablespoons
vegetable oil

I onion, finely
chopped

2–3 garlic cloves,
minced

6–8 whole cloves

½ teaspoon hot
pepper sauce or
cayenne pepper, or
to taste

½ teaspoon ground
cumin or ground
cinnamon

I cup tomato ketchup

½ cup cider vinegar

½ cup soy sauce

⅓ cup packed dark
brown sugar

2 tablespoons
Worcestershire sauce

I tablespoon
molasses

I cup water

4 pounds 'baby back'
pork spare ribs, in
sheets

1. To prepare the barbecue sauce, in a medium saucepan, heat the oil over medium heat. Add the onion and cook for 3–4 minutes, until beginning to soften, stirring occasionally. Stir in the garlic, cloves, hot pepper sauce or cayenne, and cumin or cinnamon. Cook for 1–2 minutes more. Add the next 7 ingredients and bring to a boil. Reduce the heat to low and simmer for about 20 minutes, until the sauce thickens to a coating consistency. Remove from the heat and cool. Remove the cloves and discard. Refrigerate, covered, until required.

2. Preheat the oven to 300°F. Line a broiler pan with foil and arrange the ribs in a single layer. Pour over the barbecue sauce, basting to coat the ribs evenly. Cover the pan tightly with foil. Bake for about 1 hour, then remove the pan to a work surface. Increase the oven temperature to 375°F.

3. Carefully remove the foil. Baste the ribs with the sauce and return to the oven for 25–30 minutes more, until the ribs are well-glazed and the sauce is reduced, basting 3–4 times during the cooking time.

An early 1956 Elvis china figurine, now a highly valuable collector's item.

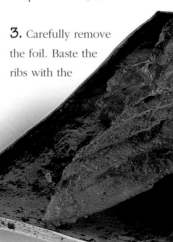

FRIED CORNMEAL MUSH
Makes 6 servings

For years a tradition in all parts of the South, this satisfying specialty has become as fashionable as Italian polenta! Serve as an accompaniment to fried chicken, roasted meats, fish, eggs, and just about anything else. Cornmeal mush and its cousin, grits (hominy grits), can be eaten as a side dish with butter or bacon drippings. In its "soft form," almost like mashed potatoes, it is often served as a breakfast cereal or side dish. The more butter and cheese added in the recipe, the softer the texture will be. Use the smaller quantities if frying or broiling the cornmeal mush.

CORNMEAL MUSH

1 cup cornmeal

1½ teaspoons salt

4 cups cold water

FRIED CORNMEAL MUSH

Vegetable oil, for greasing

Cornmeal Mush

2–4 tablespoons butter

½–1 cup grated sharp cheddar or Monterey Jack cheese (optional)

2 tablespoons finely chopped green onions (scallions)

½ teaspoon hot sauce, or to taste

Bacon drippings or oil, for frying

1. To prepare the cornmeal mush, put the cornmeal and salt in a 2-cup measure or medium bowl and stir in 1 cup of cold water. Put 3 cups of water into a large, heavy-bottomed saucepan and bring to a boil. Gradually stir in the cornmeal water mixture, scraping the side of the jug or bowl. Bring back to a boil.

2. Simmer over medium heat until thickened and beginning to pull away from the bottom of the pan. Serve as a breakfast cereal with milk and sugar or as a side dish.

3. For the fried cornmeal mush, lightly grease a small jelly roll pan. Prepare the cornmeal mush and stir in the butter, grated cheese, if using, chopped green onions (scallions), and hot sauce. Pour into the pan, spread to a thickness of about ½ inch, and cool. Refrigerate, covered, for 2 hours or overnight.

4. Cut the chilled cornmeal mush into wedges or squares. Pour enough drippings or oil into a heavy-bottomed skillet or frying pan to cover the bottom. Heat over medium-high heat and add the cornmeal wedges or squares. Cook for 2–3 minutes, until hot and golden, adding additional drippings if necessary—work in batches if necessary. Serve hot or warm.

CHICKEN-FRIED STEAK WITH GRAVY
Makes 4 servings

This is a classic southern recipe found in roadhouse cafés and diners throughout the South. No one knows how this beef recipe came to be called "chicken-fried" except that it is floured and deep fried like Southern Fried Chicken. If you like, serve with Mashed Potatoes (page 74).

⅓ cup all-purpose flour

½ teaspoon onion salt

¼ teaspoon cayenne pepper

Freshly ground black pepper

4 steaks such as top sirloin, at least 8 ounces each and ¾-inch thick, well trimmed of any fat

I garlic clove, cut in half

Vegetable oil, for frying

I cup half and half or whipping cream

Salt

Mashed Potatoes (page 74), to serve (optional)

I. Put the flour, onion salt, cayenne, and a few grinds of black pepper into a heavy-duty plastic freezer bag and shake to mix.

2. Put the steaks on a sturdy work surface and pound with a meat tenderizer to a thickness of under ½ inch. Rub both sides of each steak with the garlic and drop the steaks, one at a time, into the flour mixture. Twist the bag to close and shake to coat completely. Remove the steaks from the bag, shake off any excess flour, and set on a baking sheet or plate.

3. Meanwhile, in a large, deep iron skillet or heavy-bottomed, deep frying pan, heat ¼–½ inch of vegetable oil to 350°F and add the steaks, working in batches if necessary. Cook for 4–8 minutes, until well browned on each side, depending on the desired degree of doneness. Remove the steaks to a plate and keep warm.

4. Pour off all but 1 tablespoon of the oil and add 1 tablespoon of the coating flour to the drippings, stirring the mixture until it begins to brown. Gradually stir in the half and half or whipping cream, scraping up any brown bits from the bottom of the pan. Bring to a boil and simmer until the gravy thickens. Season with salt and pepper and serve poured over the steaks.

HAM STEAKS WITH RED-EYE GRAVY
Makes 2 servings

One of the traditional southern truckstop recipes is a simply grilled or fried ham steak, served with an ink-tinged gravy made with, yes, black coffee. The red-eye gravy is simply ham gravy and water cooled down, the pink of the ham stock giving it a pink color. Somewhere along the line, left over black coffee was added.

2 fully-cooked ham steaks or slices cooked country ham, about ¼-inch thick

½ cup black coffee

1 teaspoon brown sugar

1. Using kitchen scissors or a sharp knife, cut off any rind from the ham and discard. Trim the excess fat, leaving a narrow margin. Reserve about 1 tablespoon of the clean white fat. Snip the edges of the steaks or slices.

2. Put the reserved fat in a heavy iron skillet and heat over medium fat until the fat melts and begins to splutter. Add the ham steaks or slices and cook for 2–3 minutes, until golden. Turn and cook the other side for about 2 minutes more, until brown.

Remove to a plate and keep warm. Remove any solid pieces of fat.

3. Add the coffee and sugar to the pan and bring to a boil, stirring up any browned bits from the bottom. Simmer for 2–3 minutes, until slightly thickened, and spoon over the ham.

HASH-BROWN POTATOES
Makes 4–6 servings

4-6 tablespoons bacon drippings, lard, or butter

8 medium waxy potatoes, boiled, peeled, and quartered

1 onion, finely chopped (optional)

Salt and freshly ground black pepper

1. In a large, heavy iron skillet over medium-high heat, heat 4 tablespoons of the fat until sizzling. If using, add the onion and cook for about 2 minutes, until beginning to turn golden, stirring.

2. Add the potatoes. Using the edge of a pancake turner, chop and turn the potatoes until they form a thick, even layer. Cook for 5–6 minutes, without stirring, until a crisp brown crust forms on the bottom. Add more fat, lifting the side of the potato to let it run under the crust. Season the top. Cover for 2–3 minutes to heat through thoroughly.

LEMON MERINGUE PIE
Makes one 9-inch pie

Still served in diners and cafés from coast to coast, this delicious old-fashioned pie was one of Elvis's favorites.

Piecrust dough (page 24)

⅓ cup cornstarch

⅛ teaspoon salt

1¼ cups sugar

1½ cups water

4 eggs, separated

1 tablespoon butter, diced

Grated zest of 1 large lemon

½ cup freshly squeezed lemon juice (2–3 lemons)

¼ teaspoon cream of tartar

1. Prepare the piecrust and line a 9-inch pie plate as for Pecan Pie, page 24. Preheat the oven to 400°F and blind bake the piecrust. Cut a piece of foil 11 inches in diameter and press onto the bottom and up the side of the lined pie plate. Fill with dried beans, spreading evenly over the bottom and up the side. Bake for 10 minutes, until the edge begins to brown. Remove to a heatproof surface and carefully remove the foil and beans. Prick the bottom of the pastry with a fork and bake for 5–10 minutes more, until golden and the bottom looks set. Remove to a wire rack to cool. Reduce the oven temperature to 375°F.

2. In a medium saucepan, combine the cornstarch, salt, and ¾ cup sugar.

Gradually stir in the water and bring to a boil over medium-high heat, stirring constantly, until the mixture is thickened. Boil for 1 minute more.

3. In a small bowl, beat the egg yolks. Stir in a little of the hot cornstarch mixture, then stir the egg mixture back into the cornstarch mixture in the saucepan and return to the heat. Cook over medium-low heat, stirring constantly and rapidly to prevent lumping, for about 2 minutes, until the mixture is very thick. Remove from the heat and beat in the butter, then gradually stir in the lemon zest and juice and pour into the prepared pie plate.

4. In a medium bowl, using an electric mixer, beat the egg whites and cream of tartar until soft peaks form. Sprinkle in the remaining ½ cup of sugar, a tablespoon at a

time, beating well after each addition, until the whites form stiff peaks and the sugar is completely dissolved. Test the meringue by rubbing a small amount between your thumb and index finger—it should feel smooth, not gritty.

5. Spoon the meringue onto the warm lemon mixture, spreading to the edge of the crust to seal. Swirl with the back of a spoon to form a decorative pattern. Bake for about 10 minutes, until the meringue is just golden. Transfer to a wire rack to cool completely. Serve the same day.

BANANA CREAM PIE
Makes one 9-inch pie

Elvis loved bananas and just about anything made with them. This is a classic dish and is still found in many roadside restaurants and diners.

Piecrust dough
(page 24)

FILLING
½ cup sugar
¼ cup cornstarch
¼ teaspoon salt
1½ cups half and half
or whipping cream
1 cup milk
3 egg yolks, well
beaten
2 teaspoons vanilla
extract

1 tablespoon butter
or margarine
1 cup heavy or
whipping cream
2–4 tablespoons
superfine sugar,
or to taste
2 medium ripe
bananas
Lemon juice

1. Prepare the piecrust dough (page 24) and line the pie plate as directed. Blind bake (page 38) and set aside to cool.

2. To prepare the filling, stir together the sugar, cornstarch, and salt in a large, heavy-bottomed saucepan. Gradually whisk in the half and half or cream and milk until well blended. Bring to a boil over medium-high heat, stirring constantly. Boil for 1 minute, stirring occasionally. Remove the pan from the heat and reduce the heat to medium-low. Gradually whisk the beaten egg yolks into the hot milk mixture until well blended.

3. Return the saucepan to the heat and cook until the mixture thickens and comes back to a boil, beating constantly. Remove from the heat and stir in the vanilla extract and butter or margarine. Pour into a large bowl and press a piece of plastic wrap against the surface of the filling—this prevents a skin forming. Cool, then refrigerate for about 1 hour, until just beginning to set.

4. Beat the cream with enough sugar to slightly sweeten. Fold half the whipped cream into the filling. Slice the bananas and cover the bottom of the piecrust with about half the slices, overlapping them if necessary. Pour over the filling and smooth evenly. Toss the remaining banana slices in lemon juice and arrange on top. Spoon or pipe the remaining cream around the edge. Refrigerate for about 2 hours, until set.

39

"HEARTBREAK HOTEL"

Elvis spent an inordinate proportion of his life living in hotels. At first it was cheap motels and grim hotels. In these flop houses, the food in the coffee shop or from room service—if it existed at all—was little better, and at times considerably worse, than the truckstop and diner fare. It's little wonder Elvis spent long hours on the phone with his mother, probably remembering her home cooking. With fame, the quality of hotel accommodation and cuisine on offer took a quantum leap forward. Even in a top-class hotel, however, the potential for creating hysteria among the other diners still meant that Elvis ate most of his meals in his room. While shooting a movie on location or, later, while touring throughout the USA, the meals wheeled in by deferential waiters largely consisted of classic "comfort food." Now and then, Elvis might turn the page on the menu and become a little more adventurous.

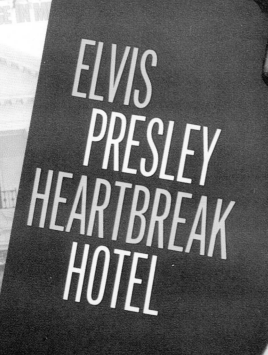

ELVIS
PRESLEY
HEARTBREAK
HOTEL

RCA

45 E.P.
RCX 7189
A "NEW ORTHOPHONIC" HIGH FIDELITY RECORDING

LAS VEGAS SANDWICH
Makes 2 sandwiches

This is the perfect sandwich—just the right combination of roast chicken or turkey breast, crispy bacon, sliced tomato, and lettuce. For a deluxe version, found on room service menus, add Swiss cheese and avocado and a homemade or "seasoned" mayonnaise.

MAYONNAISE
½ cup mayonnaise (preferably homemade)

1 tablespoon lemon juice

1 teaspon sugar

2 tablespoons chopped capers or pickles

2 tablespoons chopped fresh chives

2–3 dashes hot pepper sauce

6 slices country-style white bread, lightly toasted

6 ounces cooked chicken or turkey breast slices

2 ripe tomatoes

8 lettuce leaves

12 slices bacon, cooked until very crisp

4 thin slices Swiss or Gruyère cheese

½ small avocado, thinly sliced

Parsley, to decorate

Frilly cocktail sticks and pimento-stuffed olives, for assembly

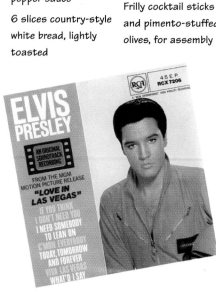

1. To prepare the mayonnaise, in a small bowl combine all the ingredients and season with hot pepper sauce.

2. Lay the toasted bread slices on a work surface and spread evenly with the mayonnaise. Top 2 of the slices with equal amounts of chicken or turkey slices. Cover each with a few slices of tomato, then the lettuce leaves, and half the bacon. Cover each with another piece of toast, mayonnaise side up. Cover the toast with equal amounts of the cheese and avocado and a few more lettuce leaves. Top with the remaining tomato and bacon slices and the remaining lettuce. Place the remaining toast slices, mayonnaise side down, pressing down lightly to seal.

3. Spear a stuffed olive on each of 4 frilly cocktail sticks.

Secure the sandwich with a cocktail stick in each of the 4 corners and carefully cut into quarters. Transfer to individual plates and decorate with sprigs of parsley.

KING CREOLE CHICKEN & AVOCADO MELT
Makes 2 sandwiches

Deluxe sandwiches of all kinds were always on hotel room service menus. Just about any sandwich can be made into a melt by adding your favorite cheese and broiling or pan grilling until it melts. Using a frying pan or griddle gives the closest result to a professional "melt" made on a restaurant "flat-top."

DRESSING

¼ cup mayonnaise

¼ cup ketchup or chili sauce or taco sauce

1 green onion (scallion), finely chopped

4 slices white bread

5 tablespoons butter, softened

10 ounces cooked sliced chicken

1 ripe avocado, sliced

1 tomato, thinly sliced

4 large slices cheddar or Swiss cheese

Potato chips, to serve (optional)

1. To prepare the dressing, in a small bowl, combine all the dressing ingredients and set aside.

2. Lay the slices of bread on a work surface and evenly butter both sides with about 4 tablespoons of butter. Arrange the sliced chicken on 2 slices of bread and spread with a half of the dressing. Cover with the avocado and tomato slices and spread over the remaining dressing. Place 2 slices of cheese on top of each sandwich and cover each with the remaining slices of bread, pressing lightly to seal the sandwiches.

3. In a large frying pan or griddle over medium-high heat,

A selection of menus from Elvis's Las Vegas shows, from 1971 to 1974.

heat the remaining butter until sizzling. Add the sandwiches and fry for about 2 minutes, until golden. Carefully turn and fry the other side for about 1 minute more, just until the cheese melts and the bread is toasted. If you like, serve with potato chips.

HEARTBREAK HOTEL HERO
Makes 2–4 servings

Elvis discovered a peanut butter, jelly, and bacon hero sandwich, known as "Fools' Gold" because of its size and its price, in a Denver delicatessen, and was prepared to blow over $40,000 flying his entire entourage from Memphis to Colorado for a take-out! Elvis would have loved this Italian-style hero sandwich.

½ cup chopped bread and butter pickles or mixed pickled vegetables

½ cup chopped pimento-stuffed olives

½ cup chopped ripe olives

I small onion, finely chopped

2–3 stalks celery, finely chopped

4 tablespoons freshly chopped parsley

2–3 tablespoons lemon juice

I garlic clove, minced

1 teaspoon dried oregano or basil

Freshly ground black pepper

1½ pound round Italian-style loaf, unsliced

4 tablespoons (½ stick) butter, softened

2 tablespoons Dijon-style mustard

4 tablespoons mayonnaise

4–6 ounces thinly sliced Italian-style salami

4–6 ounces cooked ham

4–6 ounces sliced cooked turkey

4–6 ounces sliced Provolone or Swiss cheese

Lettuce leaves, thinly sliced red onions, thinly sliced red bell pepper, thinly sliced tomatoes (optional)

1. In a medium bowl, combine the first 10 ingredients and refrigerate, covered, for 6–8 hours or overnight, stirring once or twice. Drain well just before using.

2. To make the hero, cut the loaf crosswise in half about three-quarters of the way from the bottom. Cut another ½-inch slice crosswise from the cut side of the bottom (reserve for another use). In a small bowl, cream the butter and mustard together and spread thickly on the bottom half of the loaf. Spread the mayonnaise on the cut surface of the top of the loaf.

3. Beginning with the salami, layer the loaf bottom with alternating layers of meats and cheese and the drained vegetable mixture. Top with lettuce, sliced onions, bell peppers, and tomatoes if using. Cover with the bread top and wrap tightly for 1–2 hours. Cut into wedges to serve.

Covering the Elvis fan's every possible need—the Elvis cocktail stirrer!

CHEF'S SALAD WITH WARM GRILLED CHICKEN
Makes 4 servings

This is a classic American salad which probably originated as a way of using small leftovers in the kitchen. It is an ideal choice for room service since it can be ready to put together very quickly. Use this popular blue cheese dressing or any other favorites such as Green Goddess, Italian, or French dressing. Use leftover chicken or turkey, or grill these chicken breasts especially for it.

2 large chicken breast halves, well trimmed

¼ cup bottled Italian or French dressing

I large head crisp lettuce or other mixed salad leaves, well washed and dried

½ pound honey-baked ham slices, cut into strips

½ pound Swiss or Monterey Jack cheese, cut into strips

8 cherry tomatoes, quartered

4 hard-boiled eggs, peeled and quartered

2–4 green onions (scallions), chopped

BLUE CHEESE DRESSING

4 ounces Danish or other blue cheese, at room temperature

¼ cup half and half or whipping cream

½ cup mayonnaise

6–8 tablespoons olive or vegetable oil

¼ cup white wine vinegar

I teaspoon Dijon-style mustard

Salt and freshly ground black pepper

1. Pierce the chicken breasts in several places and place on a shallow plate. Pour over the bottled salad dressing and allow to marinate for 30 minutes, turning twice. Preheat a charcoal outdoor grill or gas grill, or preheat the broiler. (If using the broiler, line the broiler pan with foil.)

2. Grill or broil the chicken 4–6 inches from the heat for about 15 minutes, until the surface is well browned and crisp, turning once. Remove to a plate to cool for at least 15 minutes. Carve into slices.

3. To prepare the blue cheese dressing, in a medium bowl, mash the blue cheese with the half and half or cream. Whisk in the remaining ingredients and season.

4. To assemble the salad, tear the lettuce into bite-sized pieces. Arrange the leaves in a large salad bowl or 4 individual bowls. Arrange the carved chicken slices and ham and cheese strips on the top in an attractive pattern. Arrange the cherry tomato and egg quarters among the meats and cheese and sprinkle with the green onions (scallions). Drizzle with the creamy dressing.

EASY PORK BURRITOS
Makes 4–6 servings

Elvis discovered burritos during his early tours of Texas cities and small towns. This was an ideal snack for Elvis; tasty, meaty finger-food. This recipe is not authentic, but it's quick, easy, and delicious. Elvis wasn't a "bean man," but you can add them if you like.

4–6 large flour tortillas

2–3 tablespoons vegetable oil

1 onion, coarsely chopped

1 red or green bell pepper, chopped

1 garlic clove, minced

1½ pounds boneless pork loin, cut into thin strips

Salt and cayenne pepper, to taste

½ teaspoon ground cumin

1 (11-ounce) can sweetcorn kernels, drained

1 (14-ounce) can red kidney beans, drained (optional)

2 ripe tomatoes, chopped

TO SERVE
A choice of the following accompaniments: bottled taco sauce, sliced avocado, sliced red onion, shredded lettuce, grated Monterey Jack cheese, and sour cream

1. Preheat the oven to 350°F. Stack the flour tortillas on a large sheet of foil and wrap tightly. Put on a baking sheet and heat in the oven for about 15 minutes.

2. Meanwhile, in a large, heavy-bottomed skillet or wok over medium-high heat, heat 2 tablespoons of the oil. Add the onion, bell pepper, and garlic and stir-fry for 2–3 minutes, until the vegetables just begin to soften. Spoon onto a plate and set aside. Add the pork to the pan and stir-fry for about 3 minutes, until golden and just cooked. Season with the salt, cayenne, and ground cumin. Return the cooked vegetables to the pan and add the corn kernels, beans, if using, and tomatoes. Stir fry for another 2–3 minutes, until the pork is cooked through and the flavors are blended.

3. Lay the warmed tortillas on a work surface and divide the mixture evenly among the tortillas near one edge. Top each with a selection of the accompaniments. Fold the edge nearest the filling up and over the filling, just to cover the filling. Fold the two sides over to form an open envelope shape. Serve with extra taco sauce, if you like.

Above: A Vegas-vintage Elvis watch.

46

DOUBLE CHEESEBURGERS WITH MARINATED RED ONIONS
Makes 4 burgers

Above all else, Elvis loved hamburgers, especially with melted cheese. These giant-sized burgers are not only topped with melted cheese but are stuffed with it as well. The marinated onions make a great accompaniment.

1¾ pounds lean ground beef

1 small onion, grated

2 garlic cloves, minced

2 tablespoons chopped fresh parsley

2 teaspoons dry mustard powder

4 tablespoons grated Parmesan cheese

Salt and freshly ground black pepper

4–6 ounces mature cheddar or Monterey Jack, cut into ½-inch pieces

Vegetable oil, for brushing

Lettuce leaves

4 burger buns, lightly toasted

Parsley sprigs, to garnish

MARINATED RED ONIONS

2 red onions, thinly sliced

2 tablespoons cider vinegar

1 tablespoon light brown sugar

Salt and freshly ground black pepper

1. To prepare the marinated onions, combine all the ingredients in a medium glass mixing bowl. Refrigerate, covered, for 3–4 hours or overnight.

2. Crumble the beef into a large mixing bowl. Add the onion, garlic, parsley, mustard powder, and Parmesan cheese and mix lightly just until combined. Shape into 8 patties. Place half the cheese pieces on 4 of the patties and cover with the remaining patties, pinching the edges together and flattening them to make 4 thick burgers.

3. Preheat the broiler. Line a broiler pan with foil and arrange the burgers on the foil. Brush the tops with oil and broil for 6–8 minutes (longer for a more well done burger), turning once. About 1 minute before the end of the cooking time, top each burger with a few more pieces of cheese and continue broiling until the cheese is just melted.

4. Line the bun bottoms with lettuce, top with a burger, and cover with a spoonful of the marinated red onions. Garnish with a parsley sprig and serve immediately with the top of the bun on the side.

SPAGHETTI AND MEATBALLS
Makes 6 servings

Spaghetti, topped with tender meatballs in a tangy tomato sauce, is an all-American favorite found on lots of restaurant and hotel room service menus. It was one of the few "foreign" foods Elvis really enjoyed.

MEATBALLS

1 quantity Italian-Style Tomato Sauce (see page 49)

4–6 tablespoons olive or vegetable oil

1 onion, finely chopped

2 cloves garlic, minced

2 teaspoons dried basil, crumbled

1 teaspoon dried oregano, crumbled

½ teaspoon dried thyme

1 teaspoon salt

Freshly ground black pepper

1 cup fresh white bread crumbs

¼ cup whipping cream or milk

1 egg, lightly beaten

1½ pounds lean ground beef or 1 pound lean ground beef and ¼ pound ground pork and ¼ pound ground veal

3 ounces Parmesan cheese, hand grated

2 tablespoons finely chopped fresh parsley

Salt

Vegetable oil

1 pound spaghetti

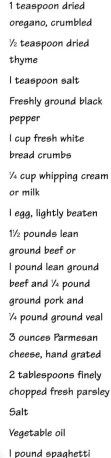

1. Prepare a quantity of Italian-Style Tomato Sauce (page 49). To prepare the meatballs, in a small frying pan over medium heat, heat 2 tablespoons of the oil. Add the onions and cook for 6–8 minutes, stirring, until softened and tender and beginning to turn golden. Stir in the garlic, basil, oregano, thyme, salt, and pepper and cook 1 minute longer. Remove from the heat to cool completely.

2. Put the bread crumbs in a small bowl with the cream or milk and allow to stand until the liquid is absorbed. Stir in the beaten egg until well blended.

3. Put the ground beef or beef, pork, and veal in a mixing bowl and, using your fingers or a fork, mix well. Add the onion-herb mixture and stir well, then stir in the bread crumb mixture, about ¼ cup of the grated Parmesan, and the parsley, mixing until well combined.

4. With dampened hands, form the mixture into 1½-inch balls. In a large, heavy-bottomed frying pan, heat the remaining oil over medium-high heat.

Add the meatballs in a single layer, working in batches if necessary, and cook for about 10 minutes, turning to brown on all sides. Meanwhile, bring the tomato sauce to a boil. As the meatballs brown, add them to the sauce and simmer over low heat for about 15 minutes.

5. Meanwhile, bring a large saucepan three-fourths full of water to a boil. Add 2 teaspoons of salt and 1 tablespoon of oil. Add the spaghetti, stirring to separate, and bring back to a boil. Cook, stirring occasionally, for about 8–10 minutes, until tender but firm to the bite (*al dente*), or as the package directs. Drain in a large colander and toss with another tablespoon of oil to prevent the strands of spaghetti sticking together.

6. Transfer the spaghetti to warmed serving bowls or a large pasta dish. Ladle the meatballs and sauce over the spaghetti and serve immediately. Serve the meatballs with the remaining grated Parmesan cheese.

ITALIAN-STYLE TOMATO SAUCE
Makes about 2 quarts

This easy-to-make sauce is ideal for many Italian-style dishes such as the Spaghetti and Meatballs (page 48), Veal Parmigiano, Baked Eggplant, and even as a base for Lasagne. Double the quantities and freeze in small containers for last-minute suppers.

2 tablespoons olive or vegetable oil

1 large onion, finely chopped

2 garlic cloves, minced

4 (15-ounce) cans tomato sauce

1 (12-ounce) can tomato paste

2 teaspoons brown sugar

1 bay leaf

1 teaspoon dried oregano, crumbled

1 teaspoon dried basil, crumbled

½ teaspoon salt

Freshly ground black pepper

2–3 tablespoons chopped fresh parsley

1. In a large, heavy-bottomed saucepan, heat the oil over medium heat. Add the onion and cook for about 8 minutes, stirring frequently, until softened and tender and beginning to turn golden. Stir in the garlic and cook for 1 minute longer.

2. Add the remaining ingredients, except the parsley, and bring to a boil over medium-high heat, stirring occasionally. Reduce the heat to medium-low and simmer for about 1 hour, stirring occasionally, until the sauce is slightly reduced and thickened. Stir in the parsley and add more salt and pepper if necessary. Discard the bay leaf before serving. The sauce can be prepared up to 5 days ahead or frozen for 3–4 months.

One of the many highly collectable commemorative Elvis ceramic plates.

LEMON-FILLED COCONUT CAKE
Makes 10–12 servings

Most room service menus in hotels have lots of cakes, pies, and desserts which can be made ahead and served quickly. Elvis loved cakes of all kinds. This coconut cake is a beauty and would have reminded Elvis of the after church "dinner-on-the-ground" buffets he enjoyed so much in his youth.

Vegetable oil spray or vegetable oil, for greasing

2¼ cups cake flour

1 tablespoon baking powder

1 teaspoon salt

¾ cup white vegetable shortening

1½ cups sugar

1 teaspoon vanilla extract

½ teaspoon almond or coconut extract (optional)

3 eggs

¾ cup milk

2 cups shredded sweetened coconut, to decorate

FILLING

Grated zest and juice of 1 large lemon

1 tablespoon cornstarch, dissolved in 1 tablespoon cold water

½ cup (1 stick) butter, cut into pieces

1 cup sugar

3 eggs

7-MINUTE FROSTING

1½ cups sugar

½ cup water

1 tablespoon corn syrup

¼ teaspoon salt

1 teaspoon vanilla extract

3 egg whites

1. Preheat the oven to 375°F. Grease and flour two 9-inch nonstick cake pans.

2. Sift the flour, baking powder, and salt into a large mixing bowl. Add the remaining ingredients except the coconut. Using an electric mixer on low speed, beat for about 2 minutes, until well mixed. Increase the speed to high and beat for 2 minutes more.

3. Divide the batter evenly between the 2 pans, smoothing the tops evenly. Bake for about 25 minutes, until a cake tester or wooden toothpick inserted in the center of a cake comes out clean. Remove to a wire rack to cool for about 10 minutes. Unmold onto the rack to cool completely.

4. Meanwhile, to prepare the filling, put the lemon zest and juice, dissolved cornstarch, butter, and sugar in a medium saucepan and bring to a boil over medium heat, stirring frequently.

5. In a small bowl, beat the eggs to blend. Pour about half the hot lemon mixture over the eggs, whisking constantly. Return the mixture to the saucepan and cook over low heat until the lemon curd is very thick, beating constantly. Bring back to a boil and cook for 1 minute, whisking constantly. Pour into a bowl. Press a piece of plastic wrap directly over the surface to keep a skin from forming. Cool completely.

6. To prepare the frosting, put all the ingredients into the top of a double boiler or a heatproof mixing bowl and, using an electric mixer, beat to blend. Set over the bottom of the double boiler or saucepan of just simmering water (the pan bottom should not touch the water) and beat on high speed for about 7 minutes, until firm and holding stiff peaks. Remove the top of the double boiler or bowl from the water, dry the bottom, and continue to beat until the mixture feels cool to the touch. Cover while assembling the cake.

7. Place one cake layer bottom side up on a plate and spread with the filling; any leftover lemon curd can be refrigerated up to 3 days, covered. Cover with the remaining cake layer. Spread the top and side of the cake with frosting. Sprinkle the coconut over the top of the cake and gently press onto the side, to cover.

FUDGY PEANUT BUTTER BROWNIES
Makes 12–16 brownies

These brownies would satisfy anybody's sweet tooth, but Elvis would have loved them—he adored peanut butter, and peanut butter and chocolate are a great combination.

6 ounces (6 squares) unsweetened chocolate

1 cup (2 sticks) butter

2 cups sugar

4 eggs

2 teaspoons vanilla extract

½ cup all-purpose flour

¼ teaspoon salt

1 cup (6 ounces) semisweet chocolate chips

PEANUT BUTTER LAYER

1½ cups peanut butter, smooth or chunky

½ cup (1 stick) butter, softened

½ cup confectioner's sugar, plus extra for dusting

1 cup (6 ounces) peanut butter flavor or white chocolate chips

1. Invert an 8 x 8-inch baking pan and mold a piece of foil over the pan. Turn the pan right side up and line with the molded foil, pressing into the corners and smoothing evenly.

2. Put the chocolate and butter in a medium saucepan and set over medium-low heat, until the butter and chocolate are melted and smooth, stirring frequently. Remove from the heat and stir in the sugar until it begins to dissolve. Beat in the eggs, then stir in the vanilla extract, flour, salt, and chocolate chips until just blended.

3. Spoon half the brownie batter into the pan and smooth evenly. Freeze for 15–20 minutes, until the surface is firm.

4. To prepare the peanut butter layer, preheat the oven to 350°F. In a medium bowl, using an electric mixer, beat the peanut butter and butter for about 2 minutes, until well blended. Gradually beat in the confectioner's sugar and chips. Spoon the mixture evenly over the surface of the brownie layer, smoothing as evenly as possible. Spoon the remaining brownie mixture over the surface of the peanut butter layer and smooth evenly. For a marbled effect, soften the mixtures for 10 minutes, then draw a dull-edged knife blade through the mixtures without touching the foil.

5. Bake for 35–40 minutes, until the surface is puffed and just set (a cake tester will not come out clean because of the peanut butter). Remove to a wire rack to cool completely. Using the foil as a guide, lift the brownies out of the pan and set on a work surface. Dust with confectioner's sugar before cutting into squares.

BLACK BOTTOM PEANUT BUTTER PIE
Makes 8 servings

CHOCOLATE CRUMB CRUST

Vegetable oil spray, for greasing

1½ cups crushed chocolate wafers (about 25 thin chocolate wafers) or 1½ cups graham cracker crumbs

6 tablespoons butter or margarine, melted

FILLING

3 tablespoons cold water

1½ tablespoons unflavored powdered gelatin

1 cup sugar

1 tablespoon cornstarch

½ teaspoon salt

1 cup milk

4 eggs, separated

2 ounces (2 squares) unsweetened chocolate, chopped

2 tablespoons rum or 1½ teaspoons vanilla extract

½ cup smooth peanut butter

¼ teaspoon cream of tartar

¾ cup whipping cream

Chocolate curls, to decorate

1. Lightly spray a 9-inch pie plate with a vegetable oil spray. In a medium bowl, combine the wafer or cookie crumbs with the melted butter or margarine and pour into the pie plate. Spread evenly and press the crumbs onto the bottom and side to form a firm even crust. Refrigerate.

2. Put the water in a small bowl and sprinkle the gelatin over. Let stand to soften. Combine the sugar, cornstarch, and salt in a medium, heavy-bottomed saucepan and gradually whisk in the milk. Bring to a boil over medium-high heat. Boil for 1 minute, stirring constantly.

3. In a medium bowl, beat the egg yolks until blended. Whisk about half the hot milk mixture into the egg yolks, then pour the mixture back into the saucepan and cook over medium-low heat, until the mixture thickens and boils. Boil for 1 minute, stirring vigorously. Pour ¼ cup of the custard into a small bowl and the remaining custard into a larger bowl, then stir the chocolate and rum or vanilla into the smaller bowl until melted. Whisk the gelatin into the remaining custard, then whisk in the peanut butter. Pour into the crumb crust and refrigerate.

4. In a large bowl, using an electric mixer, beat the egg whites and cream of tartar until soft peaks form. Gradually sprinkle in the remaining sugar, 2 tablespoons at a time, until it dissolves and the whites form stiff peaks. Beat about half the cream until it just holds its shape. Fold the whipped cream and custard into the egg whites and spoon the mixture over the chocolate layer, spreading evenly. Refrigerate for 2–3 hours, until set.

5. Beat the remaining cream until it just holds its shape. Spoon or pipe around the edge of the pie. Sprinkle with the chocolate curls.

BLUE HAWAII AND HOLLYWOOD NIGHTS

Apart from his stay in Germany while drafted in to the US Army, Elvis never traveled outside the USA. About the only places where he found himself exposed to more exotic food than mom's home cooking and the hotel room service menu was on his handful of trips to Hawaii and the time he spent in Hollywood. Hawaiian food was an immediate hit with Elvis's sweet tooth and love of barbecue, and when he returned to Graceland, the kitchen staff were instructed to take a crash course in the preparation of his Honolulu favorites. Although he rarely frequented swank Hollywood restaurants in the manner of Frank Sinatra or Dean Martin, even the fare provided by the Paramount and Warner Brothers studio commissaries broadened his horizons foodwise.

HAWAIIAN-STYLE CHICKEN KEBABS
Makes 4 servings

While Elvis was making Blue Hawaii, he fell in love with the islands, the Hawaiian style, and the "Polynesian" cuisine. He wasn't the only one; most of America in the 1950s and '60s was besotted with the "exotica" of the tropical drinks and colorful food of the United States' 50th state.

¼ cup (½ stick) butter or margarine

¼ cup packed light brown sugar

I garlic clove, minced

I-inch piece fresh gingerroot, peeled and grated

I teaspoon ground cinnamon

2–4 tablespoons soy sauce or teriyaki marinade

¼ teaspoon ground cloves

1 (18-ounce) can pineapple slices in their juice

4 large chicken breast halves

I red bell pepper cut into 1½-inch squares

8–10 fresh kumquats or preserved kumquats in syrup

1. Combine the first 7 ingredients in a medium saucepan and bring to a boil over medium-high heat. Add about ¼ cup of the pineapple juice and simmer over medium-high heat for 3–5 minutes, until syrupy. Remove from the heat and pour into a large bowl or baking dish and cool.

2. Drain the pineapple slices and cut each into 4 large wedge shapes and set aside. Cut the chicken breast halves into 1½-inch cubes and put them in the bowl with the marinade, turning to coat evenly. Allow to stand for at least 1 hour or refrigerate up to 8 hours. Preheat the broiler and line the pan with foil, or prepare an outdoor barbecue or gas grill.

3. Using 4 metal skewers, thread the chicken cubes alternately with the bell peppers, pineapple wedges, and kumquats onto the skewers.

4. Place the skewers on the broiling pan or barbecue grill and brush

A badge of the very young Elvis, issued in 1956, around the time of the release of the movie, Loving You.

with some of the marinade. Broil 6–8 inches from the heat for 15–20 minutes, brushing with the marinade and turning the skewers occasionally, until well browned on all sides and the chicken is cooked through. Serve with rice.

TERIYAKI-ORANGE PORK CHOPS
Makes 4 servings

Elvis would have loved these sweet, slightly spicy pork chops. If you can't barbecue, just broil them—both are equally good. If you like, serve with rice or lots of salads.

½ cup teriyaki marinade

½ cup orange or pineapple juice

¼ cup orange marmalade or peach preserves

2 cloves garlic, minced

4 green onions (scallions), finely chopped

I tablespoon dark brown sugar

I teaspoon hot pepper sauce, or to taste

4 boneless center-cut loin pork chops, at least 1-inch thick

I red bell pepper, cored, seeded, and cut into strips

I yellow bell pepper, cored, seeded, and cut into strips

Oil, for brushing

Basil or mint sprigs, to decorate

1. Combine the first 7 ingredients in a deep dish large enough to hold the chops. Add the chops to the teriyaki marinade and leave, covered, for 2 hours or overnight, turning occasionally.

2. Prepare an outdoor charcoal or gas grill, or preheat the broiler. If barbecuing, cook over hot coals for 10–12 minutes, turning once and basting often with the marinade, until well cooked and the juices run clear when the chops are pierced with the tip of a sharp knife. If broiling, arrange the pork chops in a broiler pan lined with foil. Spoon over some of the marinade and broil for 10–15 minutes, as above.

3. About 5 minutes before the end of the cooking time, brush the pepper steaks with oil and add to the barbecue or broiler pan. Cook until beginning to

Elvis and Debra Paget eat lunch on the set of Love Me Tender. *Elvis was seriously smitten with Debra, but it came to nothing.*

brown and just softening, turning once. Serve the pork chops and peppers with any juices poured over.

FLAMING STAR CHILI AND BEANS
Makes 6–8 servings

During the filming of Flaming Star, Elvis and his co-stars, Katy Jarado, John Ireland, and Barbara Eden, had to eat on the open range. The food brought out on the wagon or truck was as varied as a restaurant. Elvis wasn't a "bean man," but he loved ground beef, the base of this tasty chili.

2 tablespoons vegetable oil

1 large onion, chopped

I large green bell pepper, cored, seeded, and chopped

2–3 garlic cloves, minced

2 small green chiles, seeded and chopped

2 pounds ground beef

2–4 tablespoons mild or hot chili powder (or to taste)

2 (28-ounce) cans whole or chopped tomatoes

1 (16-ounce) can tomato paste

½ cup water

2 teaspoons salt

I tablespoon brown sugar

I teaspoon dried thyme

I bay leaf

2 (15¼–19 ounce) cans red kidney beans

Cayenne pepper or hot pepper sauce, to taste (optional)

2 tablespoons freshly chopped coriander (cilantro) (optional)

Rice, chopped onions, sour cream, chopped jalapeño chiles, to serve (optional)

1. In a large Dutch oven or stockpot, heat the oil over medium heat. Add the onion, bell pepper, garlic, and chiles and cook for about 7 minutes, until the vegetables begin to soften, stirring frequently. Add the ground beef, breaking it up with a spoon, and cook for about 10 minutes, until all the pieces are browned, no pink remains, and the juices have evaporated.

2. Stir in the chili powder and cook for 1 minute. Stir in the tomatoes, breaking them up if whole, tomato paste, water, salt, sugar, thyme, bay leaf, and the liquid from the beans. Bring to a boil over high heat, stirring occasionally. Reduce the heat to low and simmer, partially covered, for about 1 hour, stirring occasionally and skimming off any fat and foam which rises to the surface of the mixture.

3. Stir in the kidney beans and taste for seasoning. If you like, add cayenne pepper or hot pepper sauce and simmer for 30 minutes longer, until thickened. Discard the bay leaf and stir in the chopped coriander (cilantro). Serve the chili in shallow bowls over rice. Sprinkle with a selection of condiments of your choice.

An Elvis "hunk" key chain. The image is from the movie, Flaming Star.

ROAST TURKEY WITH CORNBREAD STUFFING
Makes 12–14 servings

Elvis spent his first Christmas without Gladys at the Army mess while stationed in Germany. He was accompanied by Vernon and may have been comforted by the traditional Christmas dinner enjoyed by American troops the world over.

STUFFING
I recipe Southern Cornbread (page 19)
10 slices bacon
3–4 tablespoons butter or margarine
2 onions, chopped
4–5 stalks celery, finely chopped
2 garlic cloves, minced
I red bell pepper, finely chopped
I tablespoon dried sage
I tablespoon dried thyme
I cup pecans, lightly toasted and chopped
2–3 cups chicken stock
Salt and freshly ground black pepper
3 eggs, lightly beaten

GRAVY BROTH
2 tablespoons butter or oil
Turkey neck, wing tips, and giblets
I large onion, chopped
2–3 carrots, chopped
2 stalks celery, cut in 2-inch pieces
4–5 cups water
12 parsley stems
2 bay leaves
2 cloves
I teaspoon dried thyme
I teaspoon whole black peppercorns

TURKEY AND GRAVY
One 12–14 pound turkey, neck, wing tips, and giblets removed for gravy
Salt and freshly ground black pepper
I cup (2 sticks) butter, softened
½ teaspoon dried thyme
½ teaspoon dried sage
I large onion, chopped
I carrot, chopped
I stalk celery, chopped
2 cups chicken stock
4 tablespoons butter
4 tablespoons all-purpose flour

1. To prepare the stuffing, bake the Southern Cornbread (page 19) and cool. Preheat the oven to 350°F. Cut into 1½-inch cubes and put on a large baking sheet. Toast for about 10 minutes, until dry, turning occasionally. Transfer to a large mixing bowl.

2. Lay the bacon slices in a large, heavy-bottomed frying pan and set over medium heat. Fry for 6–8 minutes, until very crisp, turning once. Remove to a paper towel to drain. Pour off all but about 4 tablespoons of the drippings. Chop the bacon and add to the cornbread cubes.

3. Add the butter or margarine to the bacon drippings and allow to melt. Add the onions, celery, garlic, and bell pepper and stir-fry for about 15 minutes, until the vegetables begin to brown and

soften. Stir into the mixture in the bowl, and stir in the sage, thyme, and pecans.

4. Stir 1½ cups of the stock into the skillet and bring to a boil, scraping up any browned bits from the bottom. Pour over the stuffing mixture and toss well to combine. Season with salt and pepper. Cool, then stir in the beaten eggs and a little more stock—the stuffing should just hold together but not be too wet. Set

aside or refrigerate (the stuffing can be prepared up to 1 day ahead).

5. To prepare the giblet gravy broth, in a large saucepan over medium-high heat, heat the butter or oil. Add the turkey neck, wing tips, and giblets (do not use the liver or the gravy will be cloudy) and cook for about 10 minutes, until golden, stirring occasionally. Add the onion, carrots, and celery and stir-fry for about 10 minutes longer. Add the remaining ingredients and bring to a boil, skimming off any foam which rises to the surface.

6. Reduce the heat to low and simmer, partially covered, for about 2 hours. Add a little more water if the level of liquid reduces too low. Pour into a colander set over another large saucepan or bowl. If you like, remove the meat from the neck and chop with the

giblets to reserve and add to the final gravy. Discard the vegetables. (The broth and giblets can be prepared and refrigerated up to 2 days ahead.) When cold, skim off any fat from the surface.

7. To prepare the turkey and gravy, preheat the oven to 325°F. Rinse the cavity of the turkey and dry well with paper towels. Season with salt and pepper. In a small bowl, using a wooden spoon, cream the butter with the thyme, sage, and salt and pepper. Using your fingertips and starting from the neck end, separate the skin from the breast on both sides. Spread half the butter mixture over the breast meat, pushing the butter under the skin as far as possible. Rub the remaining butter mixture over the surface of the whole turkey. Tuck the neck skin under the bird and secure with a skewer.

8. Spoon the stuffing into the cavity, secure with skewers, and tie the legs together with string. (Turn any extra stuffing into a greased baking dish and bake alongside the turkey for about 1 hour, covered with foil, adding more liquid if necessary.) Set the turkey on a rack in a roasting pan and arrange the vegetables around. Pour about 1 cup of the stock into the pan.

9. Roast the turkey for 3½–4½ hours, or until a meat thermometer inserted into the thickest part of the thigh reads 180°F. Baste frequently, adding the remaining stock little by little each time you baste. Begin testing for doneness after 3 hours. Pierce the thickest part of the thigh with a skewer—the juices should run clear. If the turkey browns too quickly, cover with a tent of foil. Remove to a platter and rest, covered with foil, for at least 30 minutes.

10. Strain all the liquid from the roasting pan into a large bowl, pressing on the vegetables. Allow to stand for 5 minutes, then spoon off as much fat as possible. In a large saucepan over medium heat, melt the butter. Add the flour and cook for about 2 minutes, until golden and foamy, stirring constantly. Gradually whisk in the giblet gravy broth and roasting pan juices and bring to a boil. Skim off any foam which rises to the surface. Reduce the heat to medium-low and simmer for about 10–12 minutes, until the gravy thickens and reduces slightly. Season with salt and pepper and, if using, stir in the reserved chopped giblets. Simmer for 5 minutes more, then pour into gravy boats.

11. To serve, remove the skewers and spoon cornbread stuffing into a serving bowl. Keep warm. Carve the turkey onto a large warm plate and serve with the hot gravy and all the trimmings.

PINEAPPLE-GLAZED HAM STEAKS
Makes 2 servings

This is a classic American 1950s and 1960s recipe using canned pineapple slices, which reflects the widespread Hawaiian influence on American food at that time. Products from the recently annexed 50th state were very popular, including pineapple, coconut, and soy and teriyaki glazes.

1. Using kitchen scissors or a sharp knife, cut off any rind from the steaks and discard. Trim and discard the excess fat, leaving a narrow edge around each steak. Snip the edges of the steaks to prevent them curling.

2. In a large, heavy-bottomed frying pan over medium-high heat, melt the butter or margarine. Add the ham steaks and cook for 2–3 minutes, until golden. Turn and brown the other side for about 2 minutes longer. Remove and keep warm.

3. Pour about ¼ cup reserved pineapple juice into the pan and bring to a boil, stirring to scrape up any browned bits on the bottom of the pan. Add the pineapple slices, brown sugar, soy sauce or teriyaki marinade, cinnamon, and cayenne pepper. Stir gently to blend.

4. Return the ham to the pan, arranging the pineapple slices over the ham slices, and simmer for about 3 minutes, until the ham slices are heated through and glazed, basting often with the juices. Serve with boiled, sliced sweet potatoes, if you like.

2 fully cooked ham steaks, about ½-inch thick

2 tablespoons butter or margarine

2 slices canned pineapple in its own juice, the juice reserved

1–2 teaspoons brown sugar

1–2 teaspoons soy sauce or teriyaki marinade

½ teaspoon ground cinnamon

Pinch of cayenne pepper

Boiled, sliced sweet potatoes, to serve (optional)

LOVE-ME-TENDER STEAK WITH RED WINE
Makes 2 servings

Elvis had always dreamed of being a movie star, and once in Hollywood he ventured away from cheap roadside eateries into slick new restaurants with his new friends and leading ladies—but it made him more and more homesick for his beloved Memphis Gridiron Diner. During the filming of Love Me Tender, he invited other actors to have lunch in his private dining room. Most of them lost no time in ordering steak. Elvis liked his steak very well done, chicken-fried, and cut into tiny pieces to save time, but his guests would have loved this.

I tablespoon vegetable oil

I tablespoon butter

2 sirloin steaks, 12–14 ounces each and at least I-inch thick

Salt and freshly ground black pepper

3–4 shallots, finely sliced

⅓ cup fruity red wine

⅔ cup beef stock

3–4 tablespoons cold butter, cut into small pieces

1. In a large, heavy-bottomed iron skillet or frying pan over medium heat, melt the oil. Swirl in the butter and allow the butter to foam and just begin to brown. Season the steaks with salt and pepper and add to the skillet or pan. Cook for about I minute, until the bottom browns. Reduce the heat to medium and cook for 2–3 minutes for medium-rare (or to taste). Turn the steaks and cook 2–3 minutes longer. Remove to a plate and keep warm.

2. Pour off all but I tablespoon of the pan drippings and stir in the shallots. Cook for I minute. Add the wine and bring to a boil. Allow to reduce by half, stirring up any brown bits from the bottom. Add the stock and bring to a boil. Simmer for about 5 minutes, until slightly thickened and syrupy. Remove from the heat, add the butter, and whisk into the sauce until melted. Season and spoon over the steaks.

63

PORK AND SAUERKRAUT CASSEROLE
Makes 4 servings

Elvis loved sauerkraut and while serving with the Army in Germany he would have enjoyed plenty of it. Use any pork cut you like—chops, loin, cubes or sausages, or a combination. Serve with boiled or fried potatoes.

6 slices bacon, cut into 1-inch pieces

4 pork loin chops, at least ½-inch thick

4 German-style pork sausages or frankfurters, cut into pieces

1 onion, chopped

1 clove garlic, minced

⅓ cup dry white wine

2½ cups chicken stock or water

4 ounces button mushrooms

1 teaspoon juniper berries or caraway seeds

½ teaspoon dried thyme

1 bay leaf

1 teaspoon chicken bouillion powder

1 (16-ounce) jar or can sauerkraut, drained and, if you like, chopped

2 tablespoons cornstarch

2 teaspoons dry mustard powder

I. In a large, heavy-bottomed Dutch oven or casserole over medium-high heat, cook the bacon until crisp. Remove with a slotted spoon to a paper towel to drain. Add the pork chops to the pan and brown on both sides for about 7 minutes, until well browned, turning once. Remove to a plate. Add the sausages or frankfurters and cook for about 5 minutes, until well browned, turning to brown evenly. Remove to the plate with the pork chops.

2. Stir in the onion and garlic and cook for 2–3 minutes, until just beginning to soften. Pour in the wine and bring to a boil, stirring to scrape up any brown bits from the bottom of the pan. Add the stock or water, mushrooms, juniper berries or caraway seeds, thyme, bay leaf, and bouillon powder and bring back to a boil. Return the bacon, pork chops, and sausages or frankfurters to the pan, reduce the heat to medium-low, and simmer, covered, for about 1 hour, until the pork chops are tender.

3. Remove the bay leaf and stir in the sauerkraut. In a small bowl, combine the cornstarch and dry mustard powder. Slowly stir in about ¼ cup of cold water to dissolve. Stir well, then stir into the pork-sauerkraut mixture and simmer for about 5 minutes more, until the liquid bubbles and thickens slightly. Serve immediately.

BROILED BRATWURST SANDWICH WITH THE WORKS
Makes 4 servings

One of the few "foreign" foods Elvis liked, discovered during his Army days in Germany, was bratwurst, probably because it reminded him of the American hot dogs of his teen years in Memphis. This makes a messy but delicious sandwich; you may need a knife and fork!

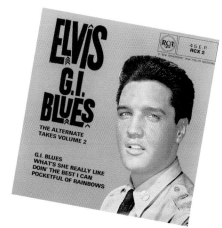

8 bratwurst
sausages

6 "hard" rolls such
as Kaiser, halved

Butter, softened

TO SERVE

Sautéed onions

Sliced raw onions

Sliced dill pickles

German-style
mustard and ketchup

1. Preheat the broiler and line the broiler pan with foil. Put the bratwurst on the lined pan and broil 5–6 inches from the heat for about 20 minutes, until well browned and cooked through, turning serveral times.

2. Slice the rolls in half crosswise and spread each half thickly with butter. When done, remove the sausages to a heatproof surface and cut lengthwise in half. Put 4 sausage halves on the bottom of each roll. Add the desired accompaniments, cover with the tops of the rolls, and serve hot.

UNBELIEVABLY CHOCOLATEY COOKIES
Makes about 18 cookies

Elvis loved sweets of all kinds. He would be in his glory now with the seemingly endless chains of commercial cookie bakers. During his Army days, he received mountains of boxes of cookies, cakes, pies, and candies from his adoring fans. He would have been reluctant to share these fabulous fudgy delights if they had been around in his day.

Vegetable oil spray or vegetable oil, for greasing

6 ounces semi-sweet chocolate, chopped

½ cup (1 stick) butter, cut into pieces

2 eggs

½ cup sugar

¼ cup packed light-brown sugar

⅓ cup all-purpose flour

¼ cup unsweetened cocoa powder

1 teaspoon baking powder

2 teaspoons vanilla extract

¼ teaspoon salt

1 cup pecans or macadamia nuts, lightly toasted and coarsely chopped

4 ounces bittersweet or semisweet chocolate, chopped into ¼-inch pieces

4 ounces milk chocolate, chopped into ¼-inch pieces

4 ounces white chocolate, chopped into ¼-inch pieces

1. Preheat the oven to 325°F. Grease 2 large cookie sheets. In a medium saucepan over medium-low heat, melt the semisweet chocolate and butter until smooth, stirring frequently. Remove from the heat to cool slightly.

2. In a large mixing bowl, using an electric mixer, beat the eggs with the sugars for about 2 minutes, until pale and creamy. Gradually pour in the melted chocolate mixture, beating until well blended. Beat in the flour, cocoa powder, baking powder, vanilla extract, and salt. Stir in the nuts and chopped chocolates.

3. Drop heaped tablespoonfuls of the batter onto the cookie sheets about 4 inches apart and flatten each mound slightly (you may need to work in batches). Bake for 8–10 minutes, until the tops look shiny and just begin to crack; do not overbake or the cookies will be dry, not soft and gooey.

4. Remove the cookie sheets to a wire rack to cool for 2 minutes, then carefully transfer the cookies to the wire rack to cool completely. The cookies are best eaten slightly warm while the chocolate pieces are still soft. If there are any left, store in an airtight container.

PINEAPPLE UPSIDE-DOWN CAKE

Makes 6–8 servings

This is one of the all-time great American desserts, which became popular during the 1950s and 1960s. For a southern boy with a sweet tooth, it was a much welcome food fashion. Use canned or fresh pineapple.

PINEAPPLE-CARAMEL TOP

¼ cup (½ stick) butter

½ cup packed dark brown sugar

1 (16-ounce) can pineapple slices, drained and cut in half, or I medium fresh ripe pineapple, peeled, quartered, cored, and sliced ¼-inch thick

1½ cups all-purpose flour

I teaspoon baking powder

¼ teaspoon salt

½ cup (I stick) butter, softened

I cup sugar

2 eggs, lightly beaten

I teaspoon vanilla extract

½ cup full fat buttermilk

1. To prepare the topping, in a 9- or 10-inch heavy iron skillet or cake pan, melt the butter over medium heat. Add the sugar and stir until blended. Remove from the heat. Carefully arrange the canned pineapple or fresh pineapple to create an attractive design (this will be the top of the cake). Set aside. Preheat the oven to 350°F.

2. Sift together the flour, baking powder, and salt and set aside. In a large mixing bowl, using an electric mixer, beat the butter for about 2 minutes, until light and creamy. Add the sugar, little by little, and beat for 2 minutes more, until light and fluffy. Gradually beat in the eggs and vanilla extract until well blended.

3. With the mixer on low speed, add about half the flour mixture to the butter mixture and beat just until blended. Slowly beat in the buttermilk, then the remaining flour until just blended. Spoon the batter evenly over the pineapple

slices, gently smoothing the surface evenly.

4. Bake for about 1 hour, until the cake is well risen and golden and a cake tester or wooden toothpick inserted in the center comes out clean. Cover with foil if it darkens too much. Remove to a wire rack to cool for 1–2 minutes. Run a sharp knife around the edge of the cake to loosen it from the pan. Place a serving plate, bottom side up, on top of the skillet or pan and, holding them tightly together with oven gloves, invert them together with a firm shake. Allow to rest for about 5 minutes, then gently lift the skillet or cake pan from the cake. Replace any pieces of pineapple which might have stuck to the pan. Serve while still warm.

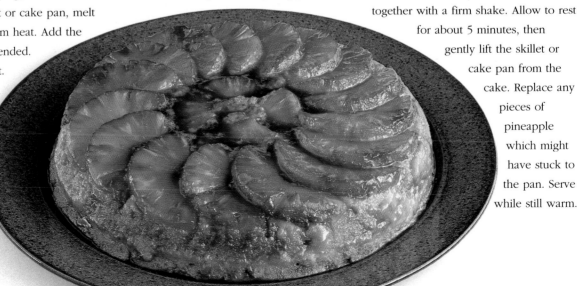

THE OFFICIAL ELVIS PRESLEY FAN CLUB OF GREAT BRITAIN

"MANSION ON THE HILL"

In many respects, the Graceland kitchen may have been the most efficient section of the entire Elvis Presley operation. While Colonel Tom Parker robbed him blind, the Memphis Mafia bickered and jockeyed for position, and Priscilla ran off with karate instructor Mike Stone, the Graceland kitchen never faltered, never closed, catered to the King's most arcane demands, and tried to present tried and tested favorites in their most near perfect form. The preparation and construction of the fried peanut butter and mashed banana sandwich, beloved by Elvis since his youth, had become such a precise ritual that, among the inner circle, it took on the sacred significance of the formulas for Coca Cola, Colonel Sanders Kentucky Fried Chicken, or the secret sauce on the Big Mac.

STANDING RIB ROAST WITH GLAZED SHALLOTS

Makes 8–10 servings

Although Elvis and Priscilla rarely entertained formally, there was a glitzy dining room at Graceland and, on the odd occasion, he would ask for a large roast. Elvis might have asked for mashed potatoes, black-eyed peas, and green beans, but glazed shallots and roasted potatoes will make this roast extra special.

¼ cup Dijon-style mustard

1 garlic clove, minced

1 tablespoon soy sauce

1 tablespoon olive or vegetable oil

Salt and freshly ground black pepper

One 4–6 rib beef rib roast (about 5½ pounds), with the back bone "chined" for easier carving

2–3 tablespoons all-purpose flour

1½–2 cups beef stock or water

GLAZED SHALLOTS

2 tablespoons butter

16 shallots, peeled

½ teaspoon dried thyme

2 tablespoons light brown sugar

½ cup chicken stock or water

Watercress, to decorate

1. Preheat the oven to 325°F. In a small bowl, combine the mustard, garlic, soy sauce, and oil and season with salt and pepper.

2. Place the beef in a large, heavy roasting pan and brush with the mustard glaze. Add enough water to the pan just to cover the bottom. Insert a meat thermometer into the thickest part of the beef and roast for about 15 minutes per pound for rare beef, or longer for more well-done meat, until the thermometer reads about 140°F, brushing with the glaze from time to time. Add a little more water to the roasting pan, if necessary.

3. Meanwhile, to prepare the glazed shallots, in a skillet or frying pan large enough to hold the shallots in a single layer, melt the butter over medium-high heat. Add the shallots and stir to coat well. Add the thyme, brown sugar, and the stock or water and bring to a boil. Reduce the heat to medium and simmer for about 5 minutes, until the shallots feel tender when pierced with the tip of a sharp knife and the liquid is reduced to a syrupy glaze, stirring frequently to coat the onions. Set aside. (The shallots can be prepared ahead and gently reheated).

4. Remove the beef to a board to rest for 15–20 minutes for easier carving. Pour off as much fat as possible from the drippings and set the roasting pan over medium-high heat. Sprinkle over the flour and cook for 2–3 minutes, stirring constantly, until well blended and smooth. Gradually whisk in the stock or water and bring to a boil. Cook for 8–10 minutes, until thickened and smooth, stirring frequently. Season with salt and pepper and, if you like, strain into a gravy boat. Meanwhile, reheat the shallots. Set the beef on a large serving platter, garnish with the watercress, shallots, and serve with roasted potatoes.

BAKED COUNTRY HAM WITH CHERRY-ALMOND GLAZE
Makes up to 20 servings

Country-style cured hams are a feature of southern cooking and Elvis's New Year lunch often featured glazed ham slices cut from a large roast. Black-eyed peas were served for good luck—another southern tradition. Old-fashioned cured hams like the Smithfield and Virginia hams need soaking, scrubbing, and boiling before roasting and glazing.

One 10–12 pound fully cooked whole ham, preferably boneless

1¼ cup cherry preserves

¼ cup red wine vinegar

2 tablespoons Dijon-style mustard

2 tablespoons brown sugar

¾ teaspoon ground cinnamon

½ teaspoon ground ginger

¼ teaspoon ground cloves

3–4 tablespoons water

Whole cloves, for studding (optional)

Fresh parsley, to decorate

I. Preheat the oven to 325°F. Set the ham on a rack in a large roasting pan. Pour in enough water to just cover the bottom of the pan. Insert a meat thermometer in the thickest part of the ham. Roast, uncovered, for 20–25 minutes per pound, until the thermometer reads 160°F.

2. Meanwhile, combine the remaining ingredients in a small saucepan until blended and bring to a boil over medium heat, stirring the glaze frequently.

3. About 1 hour before the ham is done, remove from the oven. With a sharp knife, carefully remove the rind, leaving about a ¼-inch thick layer of fat. Slash the surface of the fat diagonally and, if using, stud each diamond with a whole clove. Carefully brush over the

glaze and return to the oven for another 45 minutes to reheat, brushing with more glaze occasionally. Add a little more water to the roasting pan, if necessary, to keep the drippings from scorching.

4. Remove the ham to a serving platter and rest for about 15 minutes for easier carving. Skim off any fat from the pan drippings and strain any juices into the remaining glaze. Add a little more water and simmer for 2–3 minutes. Decorate the ham with the fresh parsley and serve with the sauce.

POT ROAST WITH ONION GRAVY
Makes 6–8 servings

Use a well-marbled chuck or rump roast or a boned and tied brisket for a pot roast, for good texture and flavor. A very lean cut will not produce a moist, tender pot roast. If time allows, prepare it a day ahead, chill, remove the fat, and reheat before thickening the gravy. Serve with Mashed Potatoes (page 74).

One 3–4 pound chuck or rump roast, or boneless rolled brisket, tied

6 garlic cloves, minced

Salt and freshly ground pepper, to taste

1–2 tablespoons paprika, or to taste

2 tablespoons vegetable oil

3 large onions, sliced

1 large carrot, split in half lengthwise

1 stalk celery

1 cup water, tomato juice, or tomato sauce

1–2 teaspoons brown sugar

1 envelope dried onion soup mix

2 tablespoons all-purpose flour

2 tablespoons butter (optional)

1. Rub the meat with the garlic, salt, pepper, and paprika. Allow to stand for 20–30 minutes. Preheat the oven to 300°F.

2. In a large, heavy-bottomed Dutch oven, casserole, or roasting pan, heat the oil over medium-high heat. Add the meat and brown on all sides, turning to brown evenly. This will take about 15 minutes.

3. Add the onions, carrot halves, and celery. Pour in the water, tomato juice, or tomato sauce and stir, scraping any browned bits from the surface of the pan. Sprinkle over the sugar and onion soup mix and cover tightly.

4. Roast for about 2½–3 hours—do not uncover. Remove to a heatproof surface and allow the roast to cool in its gravy. If possible, refrigerate, covered, overnight. Skim off the congealed fat, reserving 2 tablespoons of the fat.

5. If you like a thickened gravy, preheat the oven to 350°F.
Heat the

pot roast in its liquid for about 30 minutes, until heated through. Blend 2 tablespoons of flour with the congealed fat or, if you prefer, the butter, until a smooth paste forms.

6. Remove the pot roast to a heatproof dish and discard the carrot halves and celery. Bring the liquid to a boil and, little by little, whisk in the kneaded butter-flour mixture until the gravy thickens, stirring constantly. Carve the pot roast into thin slices, serving with the gravy and creamy mashed potatoes.

HOT TURKEY SANDWICH
Makes 2 sandwiches

This under-rated traditional sandwich is made with leftover turkey and the trimmings.

2 slices white bread, sliced about ½-inch thick and, if you like, toasted

½ cup leftover turkey stuffing

3–4 tablespoons cranberry sauce, plus extra for serving

10 ounces leftover or cooked turkey meat, thickly sliced

1 cup leftover turkey giblet gravy (page 60)

Leftover mashed potatoes or French fries, to serve

1. Preheat the oven to 350°F. Line a baking sheet with foil. Arrange the white bread slices or toast on a work surface and spread evenly with the turkey stuffing. Spread the stuffing with half the cranberry sauce and top with the slices of turkey, trimming to fit if necessary. Arrange the "sandwiches" on the foil and cover loosely with another piece of foil. Bake for 12 minutes, until heated through.

2. Meanwhile, in a small saucepan over medium heat, bring the gravy to a boil. Arrange the "sandwiches" on plates and pour over the hot gravy. Serve with leftover mashed potatoes or French fries.

MASHED POTATOES
Makes enough for Elvis or 4–5 ordinary mortals

6 medium 'floury' potatoes, about 2¼ pounds, such as Idaho or other mealy varieties

Salt

½ cup milk, plus extra for thinning

8 tablespoons (1 stick) butter, cut into small pieces

Ground black pepper

1. Peel the potatoes and rinse under cold running water. Cut into large chunks and put in a large saucepan. Cover with cold water. Add a teaspoon of salt to the water and bring to a boil over medium-high heat. Reduce to medium and simmer for 20-30 minutes, until the potatoes are very tender. Drain and return to the saucepan. Dry out over the heat for 1–2 minutes, tossing lightly. Turn off the heat.

2. Meanwhile, heat the milk and half the butter in a small saucepan over medium-low heat.

3. Using a hand potato masher or electric mixer, mash the potatoes, adding the warm milk mixture little by little until smooth. Add extra milk if the potatoes are too stiff. Beat in the remaining butter and season with salt and pepper. Serve with extra butter or gravy.

ELVIS'S FAVORITE BARBECUE PIZZA
Makes 6–8 servings

Elvis's favorite pizza was a specialty of Coletta's Italian Restaurant which was conveniently located just a few minutes from Graceland. Because pizza was fairly exotic in the 1950s, Coletta's was clever enough to invent a special barbecued pork topping spread onto a thin homemade pizza bottom. Use a package pizza dough mix or ready-made pizza dough base to make an easy version of this famous pizza.

I large ready-made pizza dough base or favorite pizza dough, prepared

Barbecue sauce (page 34) or 2 cups favorite barbecue sauce

2 tablespoons vegetable oil

1¼ pounds boneless pork tenderloin

4 ounces American or mild cheddar cheese, shredded

10 ounces Mozzarella cheese, shredded

Basil leaves, to decorate

I. Prepare the pizza base or dough according to the directions on the package and set aside. Prepare the barbecue sauce (page 34), or pour the prepared barbecue sauce into a small saucepan and heat gently over medium heat, stirring occasionally.

2. In a medium skillet or frying pan, heat the oil over medium-high heat. Add the pork tenderloin and cook for 3–4 minutes, until golden, turning to brown evenly. Add about ½ cup of the barbecue sauce and cook the pork for about 20 minutes, covered, over medium-low heat, until tender, basting occasionally. Remove from the heat and reserve any pan juices.

3. Preheat the oven to 500°F. Set the pizza base on a prepared baking sheet (according to the directions). Spread about I cup of the barbecue sauce over the base to within ½ inch of the edge. Toss together the cheeses and reserve ½ cup. Sprinkle the remaining cheese over the base and bake for about 10 minutes, until the cheese is melted and bubbling and the crust is golden.

4. Meanwhile, carve the tenderloin into thin slices, then shred the slices into thin strips. Remove the pizza from the oven and sprinkle over the pork strips. Pour over the remaining barbecue sauce and any pan juices from the pork. Sprinkle over the remaining cheeses and return to the oven for 5 minutes more, until hot and bubbling. Divide into wedges and garnish each with a few basil leaves. Serve immediately.

WHITE CHOCOLATE CHIP PEANUT BUTTER COOKIES

Makes 18 cookies

Elvis loved peanut buter and, although white chocolate chips were not around at the time, I'm sure he would have loved this. For an even chunkier cookie, use white chocolate chopped into large chunks in place of the commercial white chocolate chips.

1 cup freshly shelled peanuts

Vegetable oil spray or vegetable oil, for greasing

1 cup all-purpose flour

½ teaspoon baking soda

¼ teaspoon salt

½ cup chunky peanut butter

½ cup (1 stick) unsalted butter, softened

½ cup light brown sugar

2 tablespoons sugar

1 egg, lightly beaten

1 teaspoon vanilla extract

6 ounces white chocolate chips or white chocolate chopped into large chunks

1. Put the peanuts in a medium frying pan and toast over medium-low heat for about 5 minutes, until golden and fragrant, stirring frequently. Pour onto a plate and leave to cool.

2. Preheat the oven to 350°F. Lightly spray with a vegetable oil spray or grease with vegetable oil 2 large baking sheets.

Sift the flour, baking soda, and salt into a medium bowl. In a large bowl, using an electric mixer, beat the peanut butter, butter, and sugars together for 2–3 minutes, until light and fluffy. Gradually add the egg and continue beating for 2 minutes more. Beat in the vanilla extract. Stir in the flour until blended, then the white chocolate chips or chunks and the toasted peanuts.

3. Drop heaped tablespoonfuls of the mixture at least 2 inches apart onto the baking sheets. Flatten slightly with the back of a moistened spoon. Bake for about 10 minutes, until golden brown—take care not to overbake.

4. Remove the baking sheets to wire racks to cool for about 5 minutes. Transfer each cookie to wire racks to cool completely. Store in an airtight container.

SHORTNIN' BREAD
Makes 16 wedges

Elvis loved the rich butter cookies they used to bake at Humes High School in Memphis—the rich taste and texture must have been heaven for a poor boy. This rich shortbread, made with brown sugar and called Shortnin' Bread in the South, would have brought back memories of that treasured treat.

¾ cup (1½ sticks) unsalted butter, softened

¼ cup white vegetable shortening, at room temperature

½ cup packed light brown sugar

¼ cup superfine sugar or granulated, plus extra for sprinkling

½ teaspoon salt

1 teaspoon vanilla extract

2¼ cups all-purpose flour

1. Preheat the oven to 300°F. In a large bowl, using an electric mixer, beat the butter and vegetable shortening until light and fluffy, scraping down the bowl once. Add the sugars and salt and continue beating for about 5 minutes, until fluffy and almost white, scraping down the bowl once or twice. Beat in the vanilla.

2. Gently stir in the flour until well blended and scrape into a 10-inch tart or cake pan with a removable bottom (preferably nonstick). Spread the dough evenly and prick all over with a fork. Using a sharp knife, score the top into 16 wedges.

3. Bake for 40–45 minutes, until the edges are just golden. Shortbread should be very pale, so reduce the heat if it begins to brown too quickly. Remove to a wire rack to cool for 5 minutes. Remove the side of the tart or cake pan, leaving the shortbread on the bottom of the pan, and set on a work surface. Using a long-bladed, sharp knife, cut down along the scored wedges previously marked. Allow to cool completely. Store in an airtight container.

CARROT CAKE WITH CREAM CHEESE FROSTING

Makes 12 servings

Most of the cakes baked at Graceland were made from the newly-popular cake mixes. Sometimes extra flavorings were added, but they were always covered with a thick creamy frosting. This is a deliciously natural cake.

Vegetable oil spray or vegetable oil, for greasing

2 cups all-purpose flour

1 cup dark brown sugar

½ cup sugar

2 teaspoons baking powder

½ teaspoon baking soda

1 teaspoon salt

2 teaspoons ground cinnamon

1 teaspoon ground ginger

1¼ cups sunflower or corn oil

4 eggs, lightly beaten

1 tablespoon vanilla extract

1 pound carrots, peeled and finely shredded

¾ cup canned crushed pineapple, drained

1 cup pecans or walnuts, lightly toasted and chopped

FROSTING

6 ounces cream cheese, softened

2 tablespoons butter, softened

1 teaspoon vanilla extract

1½ cups confectioner's sugar

1–2 tablespoons milk (optional)

1. Preheat the oven to 350°F. Grease a 13 x 9-inch cake pan. Line the bottom with nonstick baking parchment and lightly grease the paper. Lightly dust with flour.

2. Sift the flour, sugars, baking powder, baking soda, salt, cinnamon, and ginger into a large bowl. Make a well in the center and pour in the oil, eggs, and vanilla. Using an electric mixer, beat the eggs and oil together, gradually drawing in the flour mixture until a smooth batter forms. Stir in the carrots, pineapple, and nuts until blended.

3. Pour the batter into the pan, smoothing the surface evenly. Bake for about 50 minutes, until a cake tester or toothpick inserted in the center comes out clean. Remove to a wire rack to cool for about 10 minutes. Unmold the cake onto the rack and cool completely.

4. To prepare the cream cheese frosting, in a large bowl, using an electric mixer, beat the cream cheese and butter until smooth. Beat in the vanilla, then gradually beat in the confectioner's sugar until smooth, adding a little milk, drop by drop, until the frosting is smooth and spreadable. Transfer the cake to a serving plate or tray and frost the top and sides. Refrigerate until you are ready to serve.

BANANA PUDDING
Makes 6 servings

This was Elvis's favorite dessert—it was always in the Graceland refrigerator. It is based on the recipe found on a box of Nabisco's famous Vanilla Wafers.

¾ cup sugar

¼ cup all-purpose flour

¼ teaspoon salt

2 cups milk

4 egg yolks

2 teaspoons vanilla extract

Vegetable oil spray or vegetable oil, for greasing

I box thin vanilla wafers

5–6 medium ripe bananas, thinly sliced

Cocoa, for dusting

Whipped cream, for serving

1. In a medium, heavy-bottomed saucepan, combine ½ cup of the sugar, flour, and salt. Gradually whisk in the milk until smooth. Set over medium heat and bring to a boil.

2. In a medium bowl, beat the egg yolks until blended. Gradually whisk in some of the hot milk until well blended, then return to the saucepan and cook over low heat for about 3 minutes, until thickened and the custard coats the back of a wooden spoon. Strain or pour into a bowl, stir in the vanilla, and cool, stirring often.

3. Preheat the oven to 375°F. Lightly grease a straight-sided baking dish and line the bottom and side with the vanilla wafers, trimming to fit if necessary. Arrange an even layer of banana slices over the bottom and cover with half the custard, spreading evenly. Add another layer of wafers, bananas, and custard, smoothing the top. Cool, then refrigerate until chilled. Dust with cocoa powder before serving with whipped cream.

Index

Acknowledgments

The Publishers wish to thank the following collectors and picture libraries who have supplied the photographs (and/or items for photography) that are featured in the book.

Michael Haywood, photographed by Andrew Dee: endpapers; pages 1, 4, 5, 7, 8, 11, 15, 17, 18, 20, 22, 25, 31, 32, 34, 36, 38, 39, 40–41, 42, 43, 44, 46, 47, 48, 49, 50, 52, 56, 57—top left, 58, 62, 63, 64, 65, 66, 67, 70, 72, 74, 75, 76, 77, 79.

Redferns/Michael Ochs Archives: pages 2, 7, 10, 14, 29, 57—top right; Redferns/Glenn A. Baker: jacket, page 9; Redferns/Leon Morris: pages 6, 11, 12–13, 68–69.

Richard J.S. Gutman: pages 26–27.

The Kobal Collection: pages 54–55.

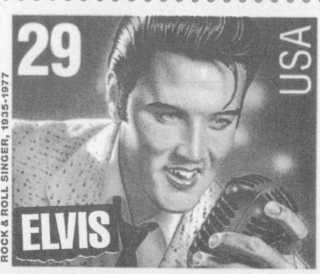